Order this book online at www.trafford.com/06-0659
or email orders@trafford.com

Most Trafford titles are also available at major online book retailers.

Note for Librarians: A cataloguing record for this book is available from Library and Archives Canada at www.collectionscanada.ca/amicus/index-e.html

ISBN: 978-1-4120-8903-6

We at Trafford believe that it is the responsibility of us all, as both individuals and corporations, to make choices that are environmentally and socially sound. You, in turn, are supporting this responsible conduct each time you purchase a Trafford book, or make use of our publishing services. To find out how you are helping, please visit www.trafford.com/responsiblepublishing.html

Our mission is to efficiently provide the world's finest, most comprehensive book publishing service, enabling every author to experience success. To find out how to publish your book, your way, and have it available worldwide, visit us online at www.trafford.com/10510

www.trafford.com

North America & international
toll-free: 1 888 232 4444 (USA & Canada)
phone: 250 383 6864 • fax: 250 383 6804 • email: info@trafford.com

The United Kingdom & Europe
phone: +44 (0)1865 722 113 • local rate: 0845 230 9601
facsimile: +44 (0)1865 722 868 • email: info.uk@trafford.com

10 9 8 7 6 5 4 3 2 1

DISCLAIMER

Do not use this book as a guide, it is meant mainly as an academic memoir. Do not attempt anything in this book without first consulting a physician and psychologist. If you continue reading, you agree to the stipulation that any physical/emotional harm that might come to your person is the sole responsibility of you, the reader. And if you continue reading, you also agree to the stipulation that the author of this text will not be held liable for any reason related to the aforementioned or otherwise.

This book is NOT meant as a threat to the reader. Think of it more like me telling you a good story.

I am a genius. Unfortunately, I'm also counterproductively narcissistic. I think that on some level I just wish that setting up the world as a meritocracy could be feasibly compatible with living in an entirely just world. Anyway, regarding my writing style: It's tempting to assume that I am unaware of my run-on sentences. That I'm incapable of formulating professional, perfectly comma'd phrases. I, full-willingly, am gonna dangle my participles... am gonna end with prepositions... weird indentations and slightly erroneous (but wholly deliberate) grammatical marks. I basically prefer my own brand of homespun gritty sexy journalistic guerrilla conversational writing that at times has to be more candid so it's easier for you to see my personality. Included throughout this book, for instance, are entries from my personal journal. Overall this book is linear, but there are definitely clunky interwoven and overlapping threads. Strange writing. Possibly exhausting, confusing. But it may be more attuned to the chaotic nature of my own mind.

Wednesday, August 22, 2007: ***Recently almost homeless due to mental illness. Even more recently, screamed and wailed ferociously in car due to emotional overload. Some days more functional than others.***

To give you an idea of what you're getting yourself into, it may help to know that one of the working titles for this book was *Self Help for the Extremely Open Minded*. That title, nevertheless, is inappropriate given that this book is not a Self Help book. Not in the traditional sense. This book *does* entwine pieces of my Master's Degree work, for which I analyzed the American Self Help industry—especially Self Help books—through the lenses of Western Philosophy, Psychology, and Neuroscience. However, I undertook that research within the context of my own self-improvement and personal transformation and fuck it. Hence: memoir.

January, 2006: ***I'm back to scratching until I bleed; I'm going to try again to stop this.***

I find ambiguity, disagreement, and inconsistency in how the term "Self Help" is used by different Self Help writers. In this book I will use it as an umbrella term with the expansiveness to cover anything from schools for becoming a pro wine taster, to cosmetic clubs for Southern belles, to pet grooming manuals made on the limited budgets of local community parishes. Frankly, the Self Help industry is a multibillion dollar powerhouse. From success coaches to marketable get-fit-fast boot camps, this business is riddled with eager patrons. It has some psychologists turned into positive-speak fascists, nutritionists reimagined as proponents of fad diets, and homemakers who've applied secrets to creating online sources of income. I tend to think of Self Help books as prescriptive conduits for the American Dream. In other words, it's as if these books have become popular—sometimes even sorta colloquial—formulas for the ideal American. They dictate how we should act and what we should aspire to be. If I take a moment to imagine someone settling in for a long train ride with their freshly purchased Self Help book… for me this is like being witness, in real time, to our very human fixation with the prospect for a better life.

Dear reader… I feel lost and crushingly lonely.

A former academic advisor of mine wrote me: "Each self-help book tends to act as if it is full of things that no one has ever thought of before. It really has a wonderful hubris, tons of optimism, and eagerness to point out how horrible we are if we don't try to improve ourselves." I mostly agree with him and can't blame him for feeling as skeptical as he does about certain Self Help publications. After all, it's so important to be grounded in a Self Help journey because the skyscraping pile of personal betterment literature can be misleading. Most Self Help books, as many of us know, promise us the stars. And yet, most of America's citizens don't seem, with spontaneity, to be spinning and twinkling as do hot balls of gas.

But, Self Help is ultimately a niche in the book industry. And no matter how it's categorized, any of said niches is usually nuanced and heterogeneous enough that it merits being branded with something besides the presumptuous, simplistic, and poorly informed condemnations that I've occasionally spotted floating around on the lifelines of academia. Admittedly, official models of the industry are fairly new (since studies of Self Help tend to be sparse and recent). Also, though the academic discussion is in its infancy, leaving room for original contribution, it is also a handicap; presenting the Self Help theme for academic consideration can itself be daunting. Steven Starker is the author of *Oracle at the Supermarket: The American Preoccupation with Self-Help Books.* He ruminates, "In fact, taking seriously the ephemeral productions of pop culture may even entail some degree of academic risk, as colleagues sitting on review committees ponder and debate whether a faculty member has sold out intellectually..." (2).[i] Tom Butler-Bowdon, author of *50 Self-Help Classics: 50 Inspirational Books to Transform Your Life,* seems to acknowledge the lack of serious academic consideration that Self Help books attract. He has a possible explanation, saying, "Maybe the genre took on its lowbrow image because the books were so readily available, promised so much, and contained ideas that you were unlikely to hear from a professor or a minister" (2).

But enough of that for now. Let's see what happened when I embarked upon my own Self Help adventure with nothing but my morbidly obese ego, a greed tantamount to pillaging pirates, and last but not least, a very sincere (and desperate) desire to change.

So, back to me.

I truly believe that the amount of effort which I've expended all these years for the sake of my own maintenance is of an extraordinary nature. And, by the way, this is more an explanation than a justification. I might have some hand in the bad that I do… and that I did. I still don't know for sure. Either way, please know that my life choices and past actions are not always easy to forgive—including those that deal directly with my conspicuous self-obsession—but that this shouldn't invalidate them right off the bat. Deep in my center I think I've done my best throughout my life given the circumstances. Every author is confronted with the gamble of losing the reader depending on how and what they present. I therefore respectfully ask for your patience, so that it at least allows you to observe my words in light of this book in its entirety. I don't want my occasional defensiveness to make me seem like a certain vigilant couple I know. They run a liquor store and always stare you down like you're gonna slip an ice cold bottle of New and Improved Sports Drink into the secret pocket of your backpack. No, I want you to feel free to stand and stretch, to roam the cabin. Oh, and it sort of goes without saying that I bring my own baggage and bias to both my writing and research. Obviously. I also acknowledge that my opinions might change and stuff. As opposed to this entire book being a perfunctory piece of academic research, I hope it becomes more noticeable as you read along that not being exclusively pedagogic can have unique creative advantages for your author.

Finally, I just want to quickly address the issue of me having a long and winding story which may at times seem fictional. This is because with me, one really goes down the rabbit hole—a sharp plummet into new, but authentic, ways of living. If throughout this book you become even slightly skeptical regarding the outlandish quality of my ways, know that yes, everything that follows is real. There are people I know who I think would gladly attest to the veracity of everything described throughout these lively recollections. Time to buckle down.

THINGS I'VE SAID TO OTHER PEOPLE

* "You're creepy."

* "My piss smells like popcorn!"

* "Wait, what did you say? I wasn't paying attention."

* "See, that's the advantage of being from L.A.—material things can make you happy."

* "Did you see that lady? The one in white. She looks like an alien."

* "In fact, you have superseded your role as dumb sidekick."

* "I'm best when I'm loud."

* "This is MINE, this is not a present."

THING I SAID PRIVATELY TO MYSELF

* "I wanna focus on me, it's fun."

THINGS OTHER PEOPLE HAVE SAID TO ME

* "You're in my personal space."

* "I suffer from information overload when I'm around you because you say so much, jump from subject to subject, and endlessly comment on me."

* "You're an enigma wrapped in a tortilla."

* "Honestly! You're a little live wire."

* "When God created you, he threw the mold away."

* "I can't believe you didn't let me share your umbrella in the pouring rain! I'm still bitter about that."

* "I want an internship in your brain."

* "You are mature beyond your years, you really are."

* "It's funny how you keep track of these things."

-Vaknin, P.222: ***"The narcissist often documents his life with vigil, for the benefit of future biographers. His every utterance and shred of correspondence are carefully orchestrated as befitting a historical figure of import."***

[The above quotation is taken from Sam Vaknin's *Malignant Self Love: Narcissism Revisited.* A slightly more detailed discussion of his Self Help book will take place in my Appendix, but suffice it to say that these quotations will be sprinkled throughout my writing, meticulously, to highlight my own narcissism.]

Cue: classical music.

What I want to be is wiser. I tend to be wise only during the most desperate of times and only when cornered into the most desperate of measures… in other words, when I have no other choice. Let's shake hands. My name is Alvaro Garcia. Al for short. I was supposed to be born disabled or mentally retarded. When my mother was baking me inside of herself, my parents had to have an adult tête-à-tête as to whether or not they should consider the option to abort, as presented to them by the doctors. My mom's tender health and age at the time were apparently not the most suitable combo for birthing. My parents decided to go ahead with it nonetheless, asserting that they would love whatever popped out because, no matter what, it was still a blessed creation of God the Almighty. As part of the planning process, they made a family pact with my two sisters that everyone would pitch in if the child had special needs; my sisters were 9 and 10 when they were enlisted. In recounting the details of my birth to me, my eldest sister told me that it was like the white pearly gates of heaven had opened up when I was born—adorable and healthy—and most of all, a boy.

My father, total Mexican machismo man, had always wanted a son that he could groom into a champ fighter or a ladies' man or anything else that might get a deserving nod from the testosterone kings. My mother says she almost gave birth to me on a horse carriage south of the border, but that I waited until reaching a hospital in California's city of Sun Valley before making my highly anticipated debut. I was born on September 14th in 1982, toward midnight, about an hour before the eve of Mexican Independence Day. Though I wasn't born retarded, I still think my family was not ready for what was coming: an otherworldly creature masked by handsome normalcy. People have asked me if my parents had planned on having me, noticing that my folks had me a decade after their first two children. I've never asked my mom and dad. Maybe I was a mistake.

My parents shaped so much of who I am today. Though this might seem the most obvious of claims, it's significant to me because I was unaware of it for most of my young life. Let's start on the maternal side of things, with a statement made by my mother: *"Yo lloraba cuando me quedaba sola y no podía alcanzar el cereal que me iba a tomar en las mañanas."* A translation from my mom's Spanish for those of you who need it: *"I cried when I stayed alone and couldn't reach the cereal that I was going to have in the mornings."* Reading this part of her letter, regarding arthritis, reminded me that she was sometimes like a cripple; she eventually had to part ways from her job doing data entry for the bank. Now she helps my father with the family business, a Mexican grocery store. Leaving her 9 to 5, which happened during my early adolescence, meant we'd be around each other a lot more.
And that we'd have a lot more opportunity to be in conflict with one another.
The rest of the family was around much less, so I essentially got stuck dealing with her excessive emotionality. I'm not sure why, but I occasionally made things worse by saying rotten things to her. I'd direct the force of my words down onto her vulnerabilities, sometimes suddenly. A couple of times she, well, hyperventilated.

(Just a quick note to mom: *Te quiero mucho, mami. Estoy escribiendo sobre los aspectos difíciles en nuestra relación, del pasado, en parte para presentar una historia más completa.*)

I think that my mother certainly could have loved me better, but not loved me more, because she has always loved me very much. But for years we were both suffering from different versions of sadness. *Tristeza.* I think my mother is happier now. Anyway, our verbal back and forths were so strange because there was always tremendous volume and rage in the air, but I was so very detached. At the time, I reacted strongly to how she looked through my things when I lived with her, personal things, and how she oppressed me with a diabolical mixture of house rules and exacting chores. Almost every day was about my mother's dominion in the house, and it sure didn't seem to bother my dad's self-esteem. She often shouted at him for making her out to be the bad guy—but she WAS in those years. She practically breathed fire. Add to that the snag that she was always nervous… she yelled in agony during the Northridge earthquake while reciting, in <u>one</u> spectacular breath, the following Mexican incantation to the highest heavens:

"Madre mía de los cielos Dios santificado sea tu nombre!!!"

When she wept during our domestic arguments, part of me considered perfectly normal the extent to which she wept. But part of me, subconsciously, always knew that it was in some way deformed. This one time, I noticed that she was obviously the loudest person at my Little League game—she was totally shrieking when something exciting happened in the match. She screamed like this, probably with tears in her eyes:

AAAAAAAAEEEEEEEAAAAYYYH

Dramatic. But, as I said, I mostly took it as the way things were… moms just acted this way. Everything was inconsistent. She'd at the most unexpected times switch from a scary foul mood to being so nice to me. So so sweet. Either way, regardless of whichever face it was that she was showing me, I've grown to see that my mom loved me during all of it. She cradled me in her arms when I was a baby and one of my earliest memories is this very thing. She even took me to Mommy and Me classes. She still loves me to this day very much with all her heart, but during my teenage years she didn't express her love for me with the persistent warmth of a cooing mother bird. (But I don't necessarily think it was her fault. She was unfairly faced with issues stemming from earlier in her own life.) As to whether or not I was even aware at the time regarding the psychological buoyancies that my mother couldn't provide for me, I remain uncertain. Also, I don't really understand what motivates her. But it is easy to notice that she is remarkably conservative. She's so religious, always thanking God for everything. For this meal. For avoiding a late fee. For the dog's diabetic status.

It's really not that hard for me to add to the description of her vibrant persona. For example, even though we rarely gelled well, there was an instance when she said something that made me think WOW that was moving and special what my mom just shared with me. What I'm referring to is this one time when she told me that, as a little girl, she was terrified of the ocean because she thought there was no bottom to it. It feels awkward—like being behind the wheel for the first time—imagining my mom as a tiny girl with little feet and little hair. I knew nearly nothing of her youth until long after I had left the nest, and even now I only know shreds. I know that she was dirt poor in Mexico, growing up in a shanty place that had a painfully palpable lack of food. She helped her mother sell vegetables. I know that she was the youngest of approximately ten siblings, I know that she was passed from relative to relative, I know that she had to labor really hard to get her first car along with her own place.

All in all, I feel like I'm recently understanding more about my mother. I more clearly recognize that she is, maybe, always so nervous about every little thing that happens (or might happen) because she was never secure as a child. She had no guarantees that there'd be some of the basics. She probably lived in a really bad and therefore unsafe part of town. This also never occurred to me, until just now as I'm typing this—the unsafe part of town thing—and it breaks my heart to imagine my mom feeling frightened of real monsters while she had little feet and little hair. It also makes me understand my old role in her story: She used to cast me in the battle against her own uneasiness and trepidation... basically, she needed me and my sisters to set things right so the world wouldn't be so full of monsters.

When I look into her eyes it freaks me out because I can tell she's related to me, that I came from her. This is what happens when you stop talking to your mother for years and then one day you see her in person again. Since you're not seeing your mom's eyes every day, it takes you aback when you come across them

again, those two dark and dewy and maternal and concerned eyes that you can't help but stare at with awe and wish you could set them aside on a table to stare at. But the need to stare at anyone's eyes is self-defeating if you don't want the person to know you're staring at their eyes. They'll just think you're staring at THEM, not their eyes. And frankly, I don't think I could ever bring myself to stare at her. Just sitting alone with her in the same room used to make me so nervous. Probably because for so much of my life, sharing the same living space with her involved a brutal and eerie feeling that she was about to criticize me. Or even worse for me was the feeling that she was about to demand something of me, when I wanted nothing more than to focus on my studies. But we've come a long way in our relationship. I'm thrilled because I plan to drink (heavily) at her birthday party this weekend, for which I am in charge of obtaining the piñata.

With my dad, I could be in the same room as him, just coloring or something. I have the vaguest memory, in fact, of just hanging out while I waited for him to pee. As far as my dad's story… he spent part of his youth speaking Mayan words to the natives perched along the Yucatan Peninsula. My father lived on a fancy ranch, had a horse, was considered a nobleman, drank goat's milk, had a chauffer, and was heir to multiple houses should he have stayed in Merida. He left it all behind because he didn't find any love in material objects, the objects which his surrogate parents (his grandparents) gave him. Though he set up a new life and now finds himself a citizen of this country, his vision of the world is still very Mexican, very macho, very family oriented. For an awfully long time he was focused on forming a legacy through his son. He would tell me that many of the males on his side of the family were named Alvaro Garcia just like him. Just like me.

Not until very recently did he stop lifting boxes of merchandise that were way too heavy for him. The man is short, but for much of my life he was super duper strong. Brute strength. Thankfully he never hit me. I can still remember times when I could tell that he was pretending to push and prod me, pretending he was so mad at me, but the truth is he didn't really feel like disciplining me. He was more interested in just being my friend. My father found himself unsuccessfully trying to connect with me for years. Sadly, there was never any kind of bond or much deep interaction with him after I was old enough to go to school, like at the elementary grade levels.

In first grade I was kissing girls while running after them during recess. A school nun held a parent/teacher talk and it made my dad so proud of his son, for being such a stud in development. (But I'm certain I did it to be scandalous, not because I was trying to be suave.) Sometimes we played basketball together—my dad and I—so this definitely gave him a way to bond with me. But eventually I played sports less and less, and in high school no one on my teams ever really

invited the parentals to come to our games due to the rather low-key atmosphere of the sports that I chose to participate in: Volleyball and Cross Country Running. Anyway, there was less and less to say to my father in the high school years when he drove me to school in his majestic, metallic, mustard-colored station wagon. He tried teaching me how to shave this one time but I got self-conscious and said I already knew how. He always told me that if I had a question about girls or girls' private parts that I could ask him, because, he said, he himself had to find out about girls and sex in textbooks. He apparently never had a present father.

He adored me when I was born and he wasn't too preoccupied with hiding how much he spoiled me, probably because the rest of the family was kind of spoiling me too, principally with attention. But he, more than the others, especially spoiled me and thought of me as a little knight or something. Specifically, one who he'd help guide to rule women and to rule toughness. He constantly told me it was important that I know how to fight, remarking that he rumbled a lot in military school. He was practically obsessed with teaching me how to box. Me, never interested. I feel really awkward when I can tell he's trying to give me advice about life and he's being all serious and fatherly and solemn with what he says, but for me, even though I know he means it, I feel like he's no Siddhartha Gautama. Nonetheless, he's quite the character. He embarrasses my mom in public and will pull stunts like sneezing abnormally loud in the middle of the supermarket in order to scare all the nearby customers. Old women in the veggie aisle were a favorite target of his, at least from what I observed. He's really slick with small groups, always goofing around with other people. He's also a hip-swaying and foot-shuffling Latin dancer when he drinks a little. I suspect he was a huge flirt with da' ladies when he was younger.

I know somewhat more about his past than my mom's, including the fact that he was very political and vocal. Also, that he was rebellious and that he protested. He was skilled at charming acquaintances, and I think if he had stayed in

Mexico that he'd be in some kind of high position or political office. I can still see this type of vitality when he interacts with his customers; how amazing he is at running a business! But the foreignness of this country sometimes muffles his spirit. It has me so annoyed, and I'm not even sure who to be annoyed at, that my dad, who likes being tough and likes being a big shot (not an asshole big shot but instead like a nice guy big shot)... it bugs me that he has these beaming characteristics right under the surface, but that here in this country the language intimidates him to a large extent. Once he gets comfortable with someone, the language trap fades and he's a fully debonair conversationalist. But not always, not at first.

It made me uncomfortable when we'd go to order fast food at the drive-thru and I could sense that he felt weak for not being able to say the words right... like, the person on the Sell Taco intercom wasn't understanding him and he'd get frustrated. He never became as good at English as my mom, maybe because he's very stubborn. She's much more American than him. She likes knick knacks and jewelry. Anyway, my signature is similar to my father's because I feel like I have nothing really to give him except for that. Maybe more of my time is something I can give him, but I don't know what we'd do. Maybe we could bowl. I can bowl. He likes bowling. Yeah, maybe that's it. Lately, the closest we ever got to bonding was when I worked some hours at the family market after I came back from my first couple of college years. He was so darn pleased to be working with me again. I didn't think I would feel the same way. But, in the end, I sometimes felt it too. Almost as if I was revisiting the most ideal parts of my boyhood.

19 RELAX!

Talking about my folks makes me think of Alice Miller's *The Drama of the Gifted Child: The Search for the True Self*. It's one of the first Self Helpy books that I read. A piece I wrote in reaction to reading it now follows:

When I think of my years as a little kid, I get really soft. I feel guilty for some reason, as if becoming older was somehow a mistake or an abandonment of something great. If not great, at least innocent. I also get really selfish with my memories. Part of me hates to admit that there is a universality to childhood... that phrases like "the innocence of a child" are commonplace enough. I get selfish because I feel like how on Earth could someone else, through such an ubiquitous scenario as a child being tucked in goodnite, understand what it felt like for me, as a little boy, little Alvarito, to feel safe in bed... being tucked in and assured that when I fell asleep that I'd be sleeping with the angels. "Que sueñas con los angelitos" is something my mom used to say to me when I went to sleep. When I think of my childhood I get really paranoid and confused simultaneously, because I feel like thinking about myself as a little kid is so personal—so much that if someone walked into the room right now (at least someone with whom I wasn't familiar) that I'd feel embarrassed... kind of as if they caught me playing with myself.

I can remember how the city I grew up in, the one I now don't visit as much, once seemed to me right as rain. The church I used to attend looks so ordinary if I glance at it now. But when I was small, the crazy bright lights inside were like the backdrop for things as they were exactly supposed to be. I didn't question it one bit. It was the church I went to. The priest—the one who sort of looked like a baseball coach—that was the priest in my life. Now I'm older, I have options. I can decide to not go to church. But when I was

small, the backdrop of my whole universe was already in place and my sole responsibility was to participate in it and rummage through it. I was, I think, more aware of small things than most of the adults around me. I paid an unreasonable amount of attention, for example, to rugs and carpets... probably because I often didn't hesitate to sit on the floor when adult matters were taking too long to play themselves out. At the store, getting one single pack of gummy worms was a fucking EVENT. Now I just throw the things into the shopping basket. My point is that, as a kid, I didn't really question reality the way that pundits and mystics do. I accepted everything. Everything.

The author, Miller, claims that any damage we suffered via our childhood leaves residues of resentment because one day we come to realize just how manipulative the whole process of childhood was for us (pg21). And more than the process, we see how certain people manipulated us while we didn't know any better. The good news is that once we see through how manipulation has left us resentful, it is less likely that we ourselves will be manipulative toward those who inhabit our current social and familial circles. I am the kind of person who you can't get to do something by appealing only to morality. I say "only" because morality, for me, just reminds me that I've had too many bad experiences being hit over the head by other people's self-righteousness and close-mindedness that I could easily have attributed to their morality. But ah, logic, logic is my friend. And the author, whether intending to or not, makes a very logical claim while explaining why we should stop fucking with other people's feelings. When we can truly work out our own shit, our own past, our own feelings—and find their true causes—we will learn how to take our own feelings seriously. This is but one step away from realizing that other people deserve to have their feelings also taken seriously. Their feelings are just as penetrating and may

have just as complex a history. This is when we can stop displacing our hatred onto innocents and instead learn to love what deserves to be loved and hate what deserves our hatred (pg114).

Miller goes into the power of childhood memories by mentioning the dreams of some of her patients (pg12). I savored these passages because they described dreams that were fairly poignant. Whether coincidence or not, each dealt with death. Each had hidden meanings, including resentment and rage. The dreams included 3 main ones. In one, a girl talked about her sisters throwing a box from the height of a bridge into a river... and said that she knew it was herself inside the box, dead, but that strangely enough she was aware that her heart was beating; another dream was of a young man who curiously examined a white coffin which he was sure contained his mother, but that when he opened it, it was him; the third one had a girl whose parents talked at her, ceaselessly, even though she was lying on her bed totally and completely dead.

If dreams can spell out the power of past images, just think of the effect they might have on someone who depends upon images for their craft. Say, an artist. Miller speculates that Henry Moore did sculptures of women with small heads because of his boyhood impressions (pg4). Apparently, he rubbed his mum's back with oil to help her rheumatism... and Miller's interpretation of this really got to me. She believes that Moore's line of sight created a specific image when he rubbed in the oil: The mother's back, being so much closer to him, looked really big compared to her head. Hence, his sculptures of reclining women with tiny heads. The fact that this type of thing could have influenced an adult artist is compelling, for it brings me back to the realization that the boy of my own childhood is not a deeply buried inner child within me. No, when I get scared, and I mean really scared, I revert. It's right at the surface. Part of me feels the same exact type

of dread that I experienced when, as a little kid, my eyes welled up after school as I sat waiting on the blue bench in front of my first grade classroom—when I honestly deep down thought that I had been forgotten and that no one was ever going to pick me up from school.

This type of feeling is of course subconscious when experienced in a present day context. But it's simply amazing how similarly I experience certain present day emotions as to when they struck me as a kid. The author reminds us to look for the child in the people who are cruel to us or hate us or who have contempt for us. At first this seemed outrageous to me, but then it totally made sense. Miller says that sometimes a hurt or despised inner child lurks behind the punches and blows (pg6). Contemplating that notion can actually get my opinions of people to be less harsh. I assure you that this is a gargantuan feat.

Ultimately, the type of sensitivity held by one's so-called inner child makes it unsurprising to me just how damaging it can be for a child to not feel loved by his or her own parents. But Miller mentions something that makes me want to stop the hefty resentment I feel toward my mom and dad: Just because one's parents didn't love them in the way they needed to be loved, it doesn't necessarily rule out the possibility that one's parents loved them passionately (pg30). This makes me feel guilty, but relieved. I am the kind of person who is quick to use criticism, but absorbing the author's idea about misguided love makes me feel really sorry for my mom and dad. Not in a condescending way, but in such a way that allows me to voluntarily put down the finger that I so rigidly have pointed at my parents for so long.

Instead of feeling spiteful for the fact that they could maybe have tried harder to support me in what I wanted to do, I realize now that there is a morsel of tragedy to the reality that they loved me soooo much. They loved me a lot, but it was like pouring milk with your eyes closed. They tried.

I think they really did their best. I usually don't want to admit that their best was really good enough. But in its own way, it was. I feel ashamed for not recognizing and celebrating the love they did give me. My dad spoiled me because he loved me. He'd buy me a toy or vanilla pastry nearly every time I did the shopping with him at the grocery store. He played competitive games with me that he knew I liked, like tossing coins into cups and glasses just like at the fair they had at my school, the fair which was called the annual Fiesta. My parents indulged me by letting me eat baby food way beyond the time I was considered a candidate for the stuff. I'd always be carried in and put in bed when I fell asleep in the car. I had swimming parties where I could invite all my little buddies.

Misplaced or misguided love during childhood can definitely have counterparts in one's adulthood though. Miller says that love is so important to a child that, if they develop into a grandiose person (like me), they will, in adulthood, confuse admiration for love (pg39). She explains that the person will never get enough admiration because admiration is simply not the same animal as love. This is definitely true of me. And quite the insight for my life. Why? Because one of my all-time biggest insecurities is that of not always being drop dead impressive to everyone. I love to shine and hate merely to glisten. I was a truly charming child, the kind that easily became the darling of an entire summer camp. Also, I lip synched and danced for an audience of extended family. Who the hell knows if this was healthy. I do know that the love I achingly needed as a kid wasn't of the kind that might leave me wanting for roses thrown at my feet. My parents failed to understand me and respect many of my choices.

The author very astutely says that when we are hating anything less than perfect, and that when we hate other people who seem to us pathetic, we are basically hating anything weak, uncertain, or helpless (pg72).

In short, the author is saying that we are hating the child in ourselves and in others. This never occurred to me. It can make me want to raise my white flag in surrender. I believed I always had the right to criticize and downright loathe everyone because you people should know better. Similarly, I don't appreciate anything lackluster in myself because I feel like I know how to do better. I realize now that I can cut people some slack, because pretty much everyone on this godforsaken planet is, in some way, vulnerable. Yes, I said it... another cliché. Many of these realizations from these Self Help books, I know, are probably cliché as fuck. I know they are. But without context and personal meaning it's no wonder they're cliché. It's when the notions hit you, really hit you and have the potential to transform you, that the cliché stops being cliché and instead ascends to genuine wisdom. At least in my (barely) humble opinion.

The author closes by talking about a book she read that made her realize that her beliefs were not all-inclusive. She used to think that access to one's present emotional tableau was possible only through a deliberate confrontation with one's childhood past. She admits that there are instead many venues, including healthy relationships and creative expression, through which one can hope to fill the holes and shortcomings left over by one's kiddie years (pg126). With a touch of Freudianesque psychopathology, she also explains that these other venues can allow for the appropriate mourning of one's inner child to take place.

Back to the Garcia family. Besides my folks there are the siblings, my two older sisters. I grew up real fast and lived a lot in a relatively short period of time because they were a decade older than me. Plus, my sisters and I have faced many of the challenges that come along with being first generation kids. The three of us butted heads with our immigrant mother for years because my mom simply couldn't grasp the importance of things like proms or sports team ceremonies—but this was more the case for my sisters than for me (since it was my mom's first exposure to such things). Aside from having issues with my sisters, like the boys they dated, my own choices definitely didn't make having American kids any easier for my parents. Unlike me, my folks prioritize steady employment and practicality over academics and experimentation. I've annoyed them by refusing to receive the Sacrament of Confirmation in the Catholic Church; have irked them by not studying something practical in college; have peeved them by being uncooperative and disinterested amidst family matters. Ad infinitum. Like any healthy teenager, I despised my parents for what I perceived to be a harsh unwillingness to understand me. But over time I've hesitantly grown to realize that so much of who they are is rooted in a Mexican culture which can be at tender odds with my American life.

Nonetheless, there *are* those traits that run in the family. There is the Garcia sense of humor. Just out of the blue, my mom once took me aside into her bedroom and showed me how she can blow tiny fizzy bubbles through the corner of her eye by pinching her nose; she said she was able to do this because of a surgical procedure for allergies gone awry. My whole family, on one occasion, got in on a prank on one of my sister's ex-boyfriends. We basically turned off all the lights while he was in the bathroom and then we all hid in different parts of the house to scare him—he was horrified by the spookiness of the dark. It's an outright wonder how my parents, traditional Catholics, can have such a funny bone. For years my dad was an actual usher who collected money for the church.

Bi-cultural living is strange to me, for I have never felt an overriding affinity with either white people or Mexican people. I will always be stamped with the fact that I grew up eating crunchy chicharrones, yet I'll always be called gringo by any single Mexican that catches a glimpse of my Spaniardy pale face. If my brown skinned kinfolk only knew what my place was in white America. For example… going to an esteemed and mostly white East Coast university was at times unsettling, especially during football games. My virgin eyes got to see all the exotic upper-middle and upper classes. Not to mention their luxury cars which were mysteriously free of bird shit. And, my gosh, their classy barbeque sets. Then there were all of the white families themselves. In the dorms, I once had a next door neighbor whose dad frequented the opera; whereas with my parents, who like to go to thrifty Chinese restaurants, my dad will try ordering tortillas because he's funny like that. I might not have Viva La Raza tattooed on my back, but I definitely am intrigued by my heritage and have done light research on the good ol' ancestors. In the Mayan section of this one history museum, I came across something called *Ullamaliztli*. This was an intense sport played by the ancient Maya, to the death, in which a human head was used as a ball. This may or may not account for my competitive blood.

Moving on. I grew up in the San Fernando Valley of Los Angeles County. At my particular Catholic school (grades 1-12) in the Valley, being me was nothing short of a phenomenon that sometimes left people with their jaws agape. The stuff local legends are made of. I was occasionally restless in class and causing a commotion. I proudly farted, deafeningly, in Mr. G's advanced (so supposedly more refined) twelfth grade English class during a slow lecture, and he immediately went to open the windows in a panic... while the rest of the students laughed or gasped, and in unison, scooted their desks away in disgust... but not without a noticeable hint of confused respect for me. Another time, I whined and slid out of my desk during a lesson—because I didn't want to pay attention—and the instructor had to stop the whole class to properly scold me the way he would a three year old. I once humped a swivel chair and rolled around on it, right smack in front of the dean of discipline. And another time I swam under all the desks. I was voted Most Dramatic.

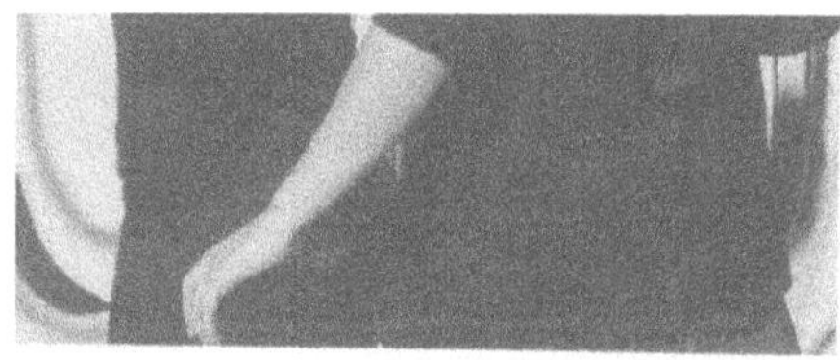

Most Dramatic

Alvaro Garcia
And

-Vaknin, P.46: ***"The narcissist dedicates a lot of his time and energy to establish his own specialness. He is concerned with the degree of his uniqueness and with various methods to substantiate, communicate and document it."***

My Catholic school was slightly ghetto, and I overheard that it was known as the "gang school" by citizens of surrounding communities. In ninth grade, some other guys in my class formed a crew called CSP (Can't Stop Pimping). Also, there was a klepto who tried hooking me up with five-finger discounts. To this day it still weirds me out to know that privileged kids from fancier institutions were taking field trips to Washington DC or fucking France while my first grade class was walking with a nun to the public library, using the buddy handholding system, as a grand field trip of the year. The entire school has changed rather noticeably since I left. It now looks like a blossoming kingdom of sorts. But at the time, as a student body, we were very aware of our rank amongst the area's private schools. I don't think it was necessarily the principal's fault, who was excellent in many ways—plus our parents worked hard to pay the tuition—but honestly, all we could do was snicker at the fact that some of our high school sports stuff was passed down, sweat stains and all, from students who maybe had their glorious heyday in the 70's. We even needed to borrow a football field for our varsity games off some community college, for you see, our own small grassy patch—a sad excuse for any kind of field—was much better suited for use by the chatty/catty girls who stood around pretending to play soccer during P.E.

[Insert here a zooooming airplane sound effect.] For college I hauled my ass from West Coast to East Coast. Partially to escape my household. The main way of financing my day to day subsistence as an undergrad was being a Resident Advisor many a time. RA's, as you may know, are the dudes that are basically supposed to live with and guide the younger college kids. I was an RA four separate times... I think the unofficial school record. Each time was its own version of sitcom. With everything that is catalogued in the university archives, nothing matches the *behind the scenes* of the dormitories. For example, one of the halls that I managed was the breaking point from which spawned a lice outbreak. I dealt with countless situations, but overall the job was pretty easy.

Additionally, my bosses were unknowingly letting me be the center of my residents' attention like an untamed hospital clown. I did a bunch of loony things. Such as inviting my residents to come see me perform as the headliner for a strip show. Or publicly announcing my sordid past as a zoophile. (Sex with dogs.) I was interesting as an RA, but emotionally gimpy… I once urinated in my bedroom trashcan instead of the bathroom because I was sometimes ridiculously afraid to see other people.

As an RA, dialing the extension for campus police was a certain kind of second nature to my busy fingers. They'd come when I had someone moronically setting off fireworks in the basement, or when I had 15-plus residents partying on the roof while I had my "panties all in a bunch." Surprisingly, ambulances and fire trucks never quite lost their novelty for me despite the fact that they got more than a few calls from us RA's. A shattered window pane of at least 10 feet in height, someone trying to pee on my door in retaliation for me writing up his friend, a keg in the large corner bedroom, feces on the wall… all part of the dormitory territory. My fascination with this kind of drama probably explains why I once almost considered working at a 911 switchboard station. I would have gotten to hear crisis phone calls.

Part of me feels uncomfortable without human conflict, as if its absence means that events don't matter or aren't important enough. I kid you not, I'm **always** in some type of turmoil. Daily. *I AM EMOTIONALLY CHARGED, I GRAVITATE TOWARD THINGS THAT ARE EMOTIONALLY CHARGED, I MAKE THINGS EMOTIONALLY CHARGED*. I find it vital for my well being to FEEL and EXPRESS a range of emotion. I just have so much angst, man. It's no big whoop of a surprise that in addition to being deemed "MOST DRAMATIC," I was also voted "MOST LIKELY TO BE IN A SOAP OPERA" when I was in my graduating year of high school. I have been known to wake people up with 4am phone calls to relieve a pressing question or comment that I might be clutching close to my breast. In the

same vein, I often can't put off making decisions because I'm so eager to move forward *right goddam now*. I rarely leave issues alone. I harp on them, like asking someone the same question again and again and again. Asking the same thing but in different ways, with my mouth virtually foaming. Sometimes I listen to the same song on repeat for hours. Sometimes I yell loudly in my sleep.

For me, it's all about the moment of impact. It's about the shit hitting the titanium-bladed fan on high speed. But my dramatic inclinations are not solely of the kind attributable to interpersonal conflict. A huge part of my passionate disposition is staked in the excitability itself. Allow me to explain. I am deeply moved and affected by my thoughts, and I easily get irritated that everyone else in the room probably isn't going mad mad mad with exhilaration and fervor while experiencing their own emotions. It just fucking kills me that everyone else in the room seems so composed like nothing. I react so strongly to things that sometimes I *literally* get lightheaded and *literally* close to fainting from not inhaling enough oxygen because I'm talking non-stop as I try to share my excitement with someone else. When I eat, I usually don't chew enough… the grub simply gets vacuumed. Also, I can be prompted to <u>sob</u> just from sitting on the couch and contemplating the mind-meltingly bizarre nature of our entire reality. Like the size of Earth as compared to the size of Antares!!!

I'm an organism who overflows out of every orifice of its body. I'm *RESTLESS*, it's like I feel this sense of **URGENCY** all the time. My mind races. Right now. Always. I FEEL what you feel when you're watching your favorite foreign film, the part where the crescendo peaks… you know what I mean, where the spine-chilling violin slices a hole into the air and irrevocably stirs up your entire emotional house of cards. This is the level to which I feel my emotions, but often without a movie in front of me… instead just in my own day to day life, and with a permanent notch UP on the dial. All of this energy, all of this intensity, is what sometimes inevitably leads me to exhibit extreme behavior. When I was a

small kiddo, I ran up and down the aisle during Mass while the more austere churchgoers pretended not to notice. Plus, this one time as a Little Leaguer, I slept in my *entire* baseball uniform—jersey, hat, glove, cleats—because I was so fucking excited about the game the next day. I couldn't wait for how my cleats were going to feel against the pavement as I made my way onto the field, how the grass was going to smell like wet vegetables, how the hurled mass of the ball was going to spank the leather on my glove. So yes, my excitement can have oomph.

I have severe mood swings. At some point I've upset or offended nearly every person with whom I've ever become acquainted. Like my mom, with whom I was obviously acquainted at birth, has received the brunt from some of my worst bouts of depression. For instance, mommy and me went through a period where she tried forcing me to say "I love you" at the conclusion of phone conversations. I worked up the nerve to protest that I should not have to say something that I did not feel at the time; probably some of the most heartbreaking words you could ever receive from your only son. Besides what I say, people are sometimes also offended by what I do. Like the fact that my best friend and I once let a street bum buy us dinner while we were in Vancouver. The bum carefully counted his fistful of coins to accomplish this.

~~~EMAILS DURING COLLEGE~~~

(Date: Thursday, November 7, 2002)

(From: me)

(To: my sister)

I did, in fact, feel like talking when I called. Which is why I called when I did. I was glad that you, for whatever reason, weren't able to get through to me the next day because my mood had slumped like crazy again. In other words, I would have probably been incredibly irritable. And about love, well, I don't love you. I don't get excited hearing from you the way you do from me. I'm sorry in a way. But, I truly do not feel love for anyone at all. Maybe a direct result from the fact that I usually feel like I'm on the brink of the crazies? Probably. I don't care about you.

~~~EMAILS DURING COLLEGE~~~

(Date: Thursday, November 7, 2002)

(From: me)

(To: one of my only friends)

It bugs me that I can't hurt you. In a way, it's comforting because I can be more honest around you than most people, without having to worry about "feelings." But, I often want to bring people down because I'm hurting so much and want to do that hurt itself justice. But then I think of people like you and I feel small when I realize that there's people out there who won't break under the weight of my words. It's good that you're working now, but, maybe I should tell you that I think you're a loser? That you haven't done much with your life except learn how to relate to your stupid dog in your own little world? You are one of the most lazy and pathetic people I know, kind of like swimming in excrement created by your inability to cope with certain realities. Hmm. I'm not sure if I feel better or worse now.

-Vaknin, P.222: ***"The narcissist suddenly becomes brutally 'honest', or bitingly 'humorous' ...or sexually 'experimental', or socially 'reclusive', or behaviorally 'different', or find yet another way to express... hostility."***

To give you some more context on these college years, let's rewind to my highly megalomaniacal teenage years. During senior year of high school, I woke up and attacked each day knowing that I wanted to become President of the United States. Though no longer the case, as a teenager I used to ***want*** the American presidency so strongly that I planned everything else around this future enterprise. Even one of my teachers (who got to know me well) seemed to believe in the plausibility of such a thing happening. This was one of the school's sharpest instructors, so I definitely get bonus points. Anyway, instead of beginning my supposed political career with City Council following high school, I started early and became Student Body President. But, oh man. This part of the story does not have a warm n' fuzzy happy ending. I won fair and square, but after being inaugurated for the high school presidency, I rigged the senior class election that I was responsible for facilitating. No one told me to. I just felt that since these students were going to make up my most immediate administrative cabinet, that I should have them cherry-picked to my liking.

I eventually confessed to the rigging of the vote in front of about half of the high school—class by class—and resigned, not because I felt guilty, but because that sharp instructor I mentioned earlier said that he'd lose all respect for me if I didn't come forward. He knew of the election ruse because I had mentioned it to him casually in conversation without thinking anything of it. Pretty stupid of me, I know. Either way, my very Catholic school was scandalized over the ballot fiasco. Many duped candidates were either enraged or stricken with humiliation when the veil was lifted. Ex-candidates were brought in for meetings with the principal so that they could be told the awful truth; I stood by and watched as a whole group of

my classmates tried to find comfort in each other's arms and frowns and tears and scowls. They were all feeling and behaving this way because of ME. To anyone who didn't know what everyone was grieving about, it looked as if the great Typhoon Tip of 1979 had crash landed into their lives and somehow taken away both their loved ones and any earthly possessions. I managed to avoid being kicked out of my high school after deliberations amongst the faculty ended in my favor.

By the time I was around 17, I was frantic to dig even deeper into my mind for any answers at all. I had to take action because, though my sociopathy had its pragmatic utility, it wasn't exactly the most comfortable state of existence. As you've probably figured out, I'm at least a little kooky. I was at one point enrolled in a summer program (located on an Ivy campus) which seemed like a bridge for high school students to the collegiate elite, but silly me had to go and get myself kicked out. In one fell swoop, it no longer seemed to matter that I was ever an overachiever. In elementary school, I went from being the parish spelling bee winner, a valedictorian speaker, and Science Fair first placer... to, in high school, being a speech champion, national essay competition winner, school talent show winner, a Mock Trial star, and having a knack for getting the highest grade in different subjects—I kept above a 4.0 GPA. During all these years, I had garnered over 85 awards and trophies. But getting kicked out from the special program suddenly made it all feel worthless. (Throughout my life I've been dismissed, in some form, from 3 types of schools. And there were 2 others from which I barely escaped the boot.) Anyway, at the particular program that I've been telling you about, I started off as a dynamic student. Slowly I became less and less functional. As a result, I got sent to a mental hospital until a parent could fly across the country to sign me out. My wristband from when I was in the kooky's nest...

By the time my college years rolled around, the focus of my manipulative ways went less to getting what I wanted no matter what (election rigging), to more of an "I want everyone to know who I am" venture. I wanted to be the most well known of the university's entire freshmen class, so I occasionally dressed up in elaborate costume-like getups... the kind that made student council meetings with administrators come to a halt. I'd combine prescription swimming goggles with fire-pattern pants and a stuffed snake around my neck. At times I donned an old lady's golden bathrobe. I even did the dual surprise of strutting around campus with nothing but a bright cape and tightie-whitie underwear much too small for my crotch area. The only way to appreciate these kinds of outfits is to really try and visualize how it was for the average passerby to, say, see me with my hat that had tiny cereal boxes fanning out in every direction from the brim. By junior year I became the self-proclaimed Orange Boy because, multiple times per week, I was clad in bright orange from head to toe... from my hat to my necktie to my shirt to my pants to my shoes. Such a thing was truly jolting to the eye, especially when Orange Boy was casually walking amongst the sea of Earth-tones-dressed-for-Fall student body. I even painted the frames for my eyeglasses orange.

-Vaknin, P.45: ***"...the narcissist seeks to 'replicate' his projected self. He becomes addicted to publicity, fame, and celebrity. Merely observing his 'replicated self' – on billboards, TV screens, book covers, newspapers – sustains the narcissist's feelings of omnipotence..."***

-Vaknin, P.139: ***"His every movement, his tone of voice, his inflection... are carefully orchestrated to yield the maximum effect and to garner the most attention."***

Journal Entry - April 2006

Having needs and desires can be so hard. I want so badly, even when I am looking at it through some of the sagacity graced upon me by my growing humility, to be able to talk to and have an audience of millions.

Besides all the adolescent image obsession during college, I was still dealing and reeling with my perpetual uninvited guest: mental illness. In addition to the mentally ill individuals I have personally encountered, I stand in the company of various men and women that I have never met. My book resonates within the tradition of other memoirs of mental illness (especially those dealing with manic depression) because I find that the emotional gurgitation of my storytelling is comparable to these texts. Indeed, even though I looked through almost all of these memoirs after I had already finished writing most of my own book, there coincidentally exist other similarities as well. For example, the clinical challenges posed to these authors by their mental illnesses are often staggeringly familiar to me. In *Electroboy: A Memoir of Mania,* Andy Behrman takes the reader through his fast paced world of art forgeries and international flights, but often returns to a discussion of mania's intoxication. He writes, "Mania isn't nearly as painful as depression, which feels like an awful storm inside my head and leaves me hopeless and despairing" (259). I have endured similar dejection.

My hypomania, which is on the mania spectrum, can be thrilling. It can lead me to do things like for no reason suddenly driving my car over a parking lot divider, or dipping my testicles in ice cream. Depression without any hypomania is definitely a worse kind of depression. When I'm depressed, I'd rather be sad because feeling sad feels a little bit romantic. It makes you feel like you're alive. In anguish, but certainly alive. During my flat depressive epochs, I have the ability to sit still on my bed without the assistance of medication, but that very action

becomes my whole itinerary. I'll sit on the nauseating bed and feel sick with sorrow… and the depression becomes all I can think about, all I can feel. Feeling snowed under. Feeling limbless. Feeling like a carnival trick gone bad.

Or, if I'm riding along in the car at night as a depressed passenger and I duck my head out the window to look at the stars, I am unable to swoon with nostalgia even if I want to. Do you have any idea how bitter it can make me to hear people talking about the pretty shiny stars? Hearing about it can make revulsion swell in my chest and skull and even in my nails. I might get wound up because stars are normally the source of magic to so many kids, having soccer mom or barbeque dad point out the constellations just like in the movie of the week. Then there's that heapload of humdrum poetry out there about the blinding moon or the soothing ocean waves. But I'll go to the beach and just feel like the shells don't love me. The sand is a nuisance. My only interest might be in determining how to maneuver seaweed down my esophagus, to yank out the bile in my gut. Anything, to feel better. Do you know what it feels like to be buried under the weight of beach mud? So much so that you're gasping for air and hoping that someone would just come along already to shovel it off? If someone pinned you down, forever, you would know what it felt like to have bricks piled on your chest… to have them there all the time no matter how badly you wanted them off and no matter what price you'd be willing to pay. But somehow I'm expected to live life this way. And if I complain too much, I'm just being annoying. Fuck this.

-Vaknin, P.117, (regarding narcissists): ***"Depression is how such people experience their overflowing reservoirs of aggression… Anxiety is how they experience the war raging inside them… It is very common to meet all four: a mood disorder, an anxiety disorder, an obsessive-compulsive disorder and a personality disorder in one patient."***

A racing mind is characteristic of mania. However, it might also intermingle with obsessive thinking. *Electroboy*'s Behrman describes a memory of running for class office as a young man, explaining that he probably appeared competent and confident because his campaign was impressive compared to that of his opponent. He says, "But inside I was suffering from a combination of anxiety and depression, dogged by uncontrolled obsessive behavior…" (13). I myself experience uncontrolled obsessive thinking intermingled with a racing mind. But my mind races in a way that I think deserves attentive explanation. Basically, my experience of time is often in that of microseconds and micromoments. Imagine 5 dots lined up.

• • • • •

When it comes to my thinking patterns, each dot represents a singularly sequential moment in time. Each of these moments is infused, absolutely infused, with catastrophic intensity. Each dot is a sliver of reflection, a decision, a moment of panic. The speed at which my brain connects from dot to dot and makes for itself meanings and conclusions (of the worst kind most of the time) is astonishing,

at least when I remember that it is definitely not the norm. It's as if my conscious mind grinds obsessive thoughts at the speed of fire. The neurons are zapping... pop pop pop. Kablamo. My mind races all day long. I often feel overpoweringly desperate just moving from one room to the next. Sometimes I'm lucky enough to have a break from my asphyxiating anxieties for a window of 5 seconds. On a good day, my obsessions will leave me alone for maybe 30 seconds at a time. But usually I'm fighting a battle all the time it's like there's no rest it's like cramming for an impossible exam every day with no relief in sight no study breaks no breathers. My mind communicates with itself in such a locked and circling and obsessed and intense manner that it makes me socially dyslexic—I was once even nicknamed "retard"—in social situations I'll basically say things to people that sometimes don't make sense, or I'll do something that's misinterpreted offensively even when I truly mean no harm. Usually I'm in orbit because there's a frenzied dialogue in my head. I find meditation stressful.

All of this freakish extreme apprehension goes on for the next 30 seconds, the next hour, the next week... until I actually do say something very rude (to release myself with distraction). Or I pop a pill that just leaves me sludgy and fried. I've been in situations where I've zonked myself so much with sedatives that I'm literally on the floor on the rug with my face having red marks dig into my cheeks from the rug and I can't get up or even move my arm into a slightly more comfortable position and my body is that weak but my mind will still be going racing and racing. I hated some side effects of code name Nox, but it was one of the only kinds of psychiatric meds that could make my mind stop. Unfortunately, this is precisely what it gave to my mind: a stop. *But not a peaceful one*. It forced me to sit down against my will and had me blankly staring at the wall like a zombie. My eyes fixed but distant. Pharmaceutically lobotomized. Head on desk in class.

My racing mind constantly seduces my obsessive mind. There's my BDD, for instance. I'm talking about a diagnosed psychological condition I have called Body Dysmorphic Disorder. People with BDD are obsessed with their own perceived physical flaws, features which to an objective outsider can be extremely minor, invisible, or even attractive, but to the BDD sufferer are emotionally devastating. Let me explain. I have this little red vein in the corner of my right eye. This little fucker was a source of my lunacy for years. There were days when it was mainly what I thought about, and it indirectly may have interfered with the quality of my academic work during that period of my life. I would not only think about **the red vein**, I would obsess. I would ask a confidante to reassure me about some aspect of my face, like **the red vein**. This friend would reassure me, saying that not only was it barely noticeable, but that they could not see it unless they looked really really hard and with a fine precision. I'd calm down a little. But then I'd run across the room and look in the mirror and hold my face about two inches away from the glass, opening my eyes wide and spotting the perpetrator. I'd again become distraught. I'd get upset at my supposed confidante, saying that **the red vein** was right there. I'd have them look at it again. They'd say, sure, now that I point it out they can see it—but barely. But, I retort, it IS possible then that someone might be able to see it! I run to the mirror again. My eyes start to moisten with impatience because I can feel my delicately balanced sensibilities crashing down before me. The older I get, the bigger and longer **the red vein** will become. No way around it.

I sit down on my friend's bed and the friend starts talking about Biology class or something. I cannot listen. I am focused on one thing and one thing only. It is my everything. That one piece of my eye holds me nailed to a big fat cross. I leave my friend's room so that I can look in my own mirror for about 45 minutes, in my own room where no one can bother me. I leave my room and eventually ask this same friend for reassurance again, igniting the debate anew. For me this isn't

something that'd happen just for those last 10 minutes before, say, school pictures. For me, it's what I would think about (and be crushed about) nearly every hour of certain days. Breakfast. **Eye vein.** Lunch. **Eye vein.** Dinner. **Eye vein.** Toilet. **Eye vein.** Shower. **Eye vein.** Changing my sweater. **Eye vein.** Hanging a coat. **Eye vein.** Hailing a taxi. **Eye vein.** Even though no one else seemed to notice it, I felt like I couldn't live a normal life with a little vein like that in my eye. I am not exaggerating! This is how I truly would feel. Like leagues of the sea were flooding down on me. I'd be at the cafeteria and it would be like a permanent thorn lodged into my brain. Into my eye. The thought. The terror. It would leave me totally empty and flustered. I might run to the cafeteria bathroom to examine it. To see how bad it was. I might get up in the middle of yet another conversation and look again. Again. Again. I think you're starting to get the point. For years I've had so many body image issues just like this one.

It was very helpful to read *The Broken Mirror: Understanding and Treating Body Dysmorphic Disorder* by Katharine Phillips, M.D. I learned that in many documented BDD cases, such flaws have led to suicide. Also, entire families have disintegrated because of one person's obsessions. It all made me feel less alone. After all, it's torment. BDD is partially why I had to stop looking in the mirror at one point. I did an experiment where I <u>didn't once</u> look at my reflection for months, not once. Every single time I walked into a bathroom, for instance, I'd keep my sight fixed on the ground so that I could safely search for the plumbing pipes of the sinks. (This usually indicated where the mirrors were.) Even when I was peeing into the toilet, I wouldn't dare look… for fear of seeing my face. If I was putting on a CD, I'd look away because I knew the surface was reflective. I also didn't allow myself to see my own image in photographs. I developed a rather interesting relationship to my shadow because that became the only frame of reference for how I actually looked. You'd be surprised how easy it is to forget how you look after not seeing yourself for such a long period. When you're a Resident Advisor

and you've got a mirror in the dorm bathroom taped up with construction paper, plus a note asking the janitor to please leave it be, there sure is a lot of confusion left going around the hall. The residents initially assumed the mirror was broken. But the broken thing was, like, me.

I've been told that I should be a male model. It doesn't make a difference. That's what sucks about BDD, no size of compliment can heal you. When a bunch of students once nominated me as a candidate for being the best looking guy in my class, I was genuinely shocked. I see something hideous, ugly, in the mirror; it makes me feel like utter shit. And if I'm caught gawking into the looking glass, folks probably assume it's vanity. But if anything could be further away from vanity BDD sure it be. Ironically, it makes you want to rip your own face off... but you can't. You'd just look worse. And I'm screwed anyway because I recently got an unsightly medical condition called Aging Face.

Back to the mental illness memoirs. *Girl, Interrupted* was adapted into a major motion picture in 1999, as directed by James Mangold. It was based on Susanna Kaysen's book of the same title, in which she reminisces about her two-year stay at a Boston psychiatric hospital nearly 3 decades prior. She pays particular attention to the nuances of mood as experienced during her stay, postulating that the terminology commonly utilized to describe negative emotional states is sorely insufficient. She says, "There are a lot of names: depression, catatonia, mania, anxiety, agitation. They don't tell you much" (75). William Styron, now dead, also believed that mood is extremely subtle, to the degree that it can snowball slowly over time. At one point in his *Darkness Visible: A Memoir of Madness,* he recounts an alcohol-related emotional breakdown: "The storm which swept me into a hospital in December began as a cloud no bigger than a wine goblet the previous June" (40). The depression that Styron fell victim to in 1985 was of the suicidal variety, and entries such as the one above come together to outline his descent into a type of insanity. In *Call Me Anna: The Autobiography of Patty Duke,* the

author keenly describes the shades of mood similarly to Kaysen and Styron. Duke writes about a common deception of positive mood, namely the illusion of permanent wellness: "What I was experiencing was one of those stable periods that sometimes occurs between untreated manic and depressed moods. I had come out of the tunnel and I thought this was the way it was going to be for the rest of my life" (176).

Other common threads I found in these memoirs of mental illness were the authors' overwhelming confusion regarding their own behavior. Styron's book echoes this when he says, "As I set down these recollections, I realize that it should have been plain to me that I was already in the grip of the beginning of a mood disorder, but I was ignorant of such a condition at that time" (42). In many instances, mental illness is not even recognized as such until later in life. In my own life, for example, my temperament as a high school student was a bit mysterious to both me and my parents. Some people just assumed I was a jerk. Anyway, maybe a foreboding hint of my sour social inclinations was the fact that I hurt animals when I was a child. This sort of thing unfortunately doesn't just happen in warped fairy tales. Though it might be impossible to fathom, I performed those acts out of curiosity… not malice. Luckily, my blind faith in the Word of God at the time kept me from ever considering something like suicide or homicide. Besides, I've never ever had a desire for either one.

Ultimately, this book is not meant to speak for all of "the mentally ill." I bet the term itself, along with its potential implications, is not even used comfortably across the board by all patients. Each patient is unique in symptom severity and type, depending on their particular disorders or pathologies. However, my academic m*E*nTa*l* b*R*eAk*D*oWn (for which I got kicked out of the program located on the Ivy campus) resonates well with Elizabeth Wurtzel's memoir. Her book, *Prozac Nation,* was adapted into a feature length film just as in the case of Kaysen's *Girl, Interrupted.* Wurtzel discusses the heaviness of her struggle while at Harvard University, and also at home: "Some days, I was so deep in sorrow that every little thing, walking across the street or fixing myself breakfast, was such an effort that I didn't even bother" (104). I too have been trampled by despondency. Just trying to keep myself together enough to stand up and get a cup of water. Just to wash my hands and then put down the soap.

Whether one comes to awareness of one's own mental illness, or is instead informed, the process is often further complicated by the proper determination of a diagnosis. I've often read of patients complaining about misdiagnosis and overdiagnosis. My own diagnosis is ambiguous. In addition to a fluctuating cornucopia of anxiety and depression, of anxiety and depression, of anxiety and depression... different shrinks have tagged me as Obsessive-Compulsive, Borderline, Bipolar 2, Dysthymic, Hypochondriacal, and Body Dysmorphic. As part of writing her memoir, Susanna Kaysen consulted a lawyer to help her extract hospital files, and she describes how she proceeded "to locate a copy of the *Diagnostic and Statistical Manual of Mental Disorders* and look up Borderline Personality to see what they really thought..." (150). Kaysen's investigation into the DSM reflects the pressing desire of many patients to find out more about their conditions. Clinical opinions and research often become parts of a necessary routine.

In my own case, I've had to consider the fact that I fell onto cement when I was a baby. Family members tell me that there was a thud, after the hammock came undone, and that I was rushed to the hospital. Even though preliminary assessments didn't reveal much, the moment when my tiny head connected with the ground has perhaps changed the course of my life unspeakably. It seems to have possibly left me with permanent brain damage. When I got older, a psychoneurophysiologist assessed me as having "controlled right hemispheric trauma to the brain"—this specialist, who said that the nature of the head injury seemed to trace back to early life, had in no way been tipped off about the fall I had in infancy. I hope to someday undergo extensive neuroimaging evaluations to see what else I can learn about all of this on a neurophysiological level. Amongst the avenues I have explored for the sake of my ever-so-slightly battered brain, I once participated in a university electrocranial study that mostly gave me headaches. Also, the earlier mentioned psychoneurophysiologist used electrodes to plug my head into a machine apparently designed for modifying screwy levels of alpha, beta, and theta waves. After years of this and other kinds of therapy, it still isn't clear to me whether my long string of mental illnesses derive from genetics, rearing, dietary/exercise habits, brain damage, or some combination thereof.

Part of doing research on one's afflictions is doing research on one's options for recovery. Each patient is different, but psychotherapy is common for patients with mood, personality, and anxiety disorders. Many mental illness memoirs, including Kaysen's, list personal routines of talk therapy. In her book she says, "Each of us saw three doctors a day: the ward doctor, the resident, and our own therapist" (83). I myself tried talking to a social worker for years. I also tried psychotherapy, cognitive behavioral therapy, and finally… and reluctantly… heavy medication. I went through 5 meds in total. During the initial months on certain pills, I had a type of daytime hallucination where I was a thick oozing slug slithering on the floor. One medication gifted me with those well known sexual

side effects; also constipation. Another med had me laughing giddily like a chimpanzee. My side effects also included: being disgusted by food, having the floor spiral before my eyes, being unable to breathe correctly, and not being able to recall basic words for things like "fork" no matter how hard I tried. I personally know a patient whose pills made her see creatures coming out of the wall; she also saw people (who weren't really there) watching her through the windows. The availability of meds makes obvious the fact that, though talk therapy is a valuable option, it is not always a complete one. Yet, even medication itself is not always considered by all patients to be the last resort. Behrman, the *Electroboy* author, at one point says, "So I ask the question about the last resort—electroconvulsive therapy, or electroshock therapy, as it is more commonly called" (221).

The options available to the mentally ill are rarely straightforward, often entailing excruciating concessions and even a possible worsening of circumstances. Nonetheless, sometimes certain options such as medication can be life-changing and life-saving. In her *Call Me Anna,* Duke describes the relief that she received from the meds she took, saying, "The only people who would probably give a bigger testimonial for Lithium than me are my kids. These are the people who witnessed and suffered the most during those times when their mother was out of control" (289). Psychiatric medication, however—even when used appropriately and under the guidance of a clinician—is a sensitive factor in recovery. Sometimes it helps to administer meds rigorously, sometimes it helps to switch, sometimes it helps to wean the patient off completely, but none of these paths is ever fully guaranteed. Kay Jamison, psychiatrist and author of *An Unquiet Mind: A Memoir of Moods and Madness,* says in her book, "By March of 1975, six months after starting lithium, I had stopped taking it. Within weeks I became manic and then severely depressed" (100). Due to the existence of insomnia in certain patients, sedatives are sometimes administered in addition to traditional antidepressants, antianxiety

agents, and mood stabilizers. Styron explains, "Aided by the minor tranquilizer Halcion, I had managed to defeat my insomnia and get a few hours' sleep" (8).

In my own case, I decided to find a route outside of meds. I've spent countless nights raking through alternative medicine resources, both in online and book format. Through an exceptionally slow and persnickety process, I've managed to wean myself off of all psychiatric medication and am currently on a combination of specially chosen supplements. I ingest around 55 capsules and tablets per day. **(Note: I went off my psychiatric medication gradually and with the approval of professionals. I am not encouraging you to abruptly stop your medication, if you are on any. Do not make decisions regarding your prescriptions without consulting your doctor. Supplements may not be the right path for all patients.)**

I went on medication in the first place because my behavior destroyed the most important relationship of my life. Whether a mentally ill person is reacting to the trauma of anxiety, depression, or obsessive thinking, the person's behavior inevitably affects the people within close proximity to them. Especially if the patient becomes physically or emotionally hostile. Duke questions someone who receives the blows of her disparagement: "How many times can I shoot a clever, witty one-liner and embarrass you before you pull the plug?" (301). The alienation of others goes hand in hand with loneliness. In an Afterword for *Prozac Nation,* Wurtzel says, "When I finally have to explain my motives for writing this book, it really does come down to wanting to feel less lonely in this lonely feeling, wanting to shed depression's thick, tender, suffocating skin" (359). In this sense, I feel that my book is not necessarily set out to do anything different than the other memoirs I have mentioned. Frankly, almost every single day, I undergo such ruthless internal exasperation that I become easily overwhelmed. I feel acutely isolated and imprisoned in my own mind.

Writing my book and allowing it to be read by the public is a process of splendid catharsis. Ironically, I'm a hermit. I usually dislike interacting with people. I find it so frustrating. And other times I'm just plain shy.

Journal Entry – JULY 2006

Maybe it's even more tragic that I'm simply unwilling to share my victimhood. I think I know, but deny, that it would relieve me from a lot of my lonely terror if I just stood up, opened up my eyes, and walked around the classroom. The cafe. Restaurant. Wherever I might be. And stopped and asked people about their pain. I'd find out that other people were unhappy too. In their own unique ways. But it's like I block it out of my mind so that I can hold onto my vengeance. My beautiful jeweled chalice full of venom that I can't stop drinking.

I'm frustrated because my emotions feel so important. But the world keeps telling me, in every way, that they are not. Other people feel shitty too. They get cancer. Lose a baby sister. Accidentally stain their favorite shirt. Lose an important contract. They kill their brother and regret it forever in a jail cell. And yet I, a stupid lonely bastard, without flinching, can feel as if my pain is somehow more of more. More better. More uber.

I'm so obsessed with myself you really have no idea. These words and the book don't really convey it. It's as if I am an inverted mirror on legs. I exist because I believe so strongly that my presence is essential for keeping the periodic table intact, for keeping the world glued together. The idea of a world without me, a human history without me, is so totally absurd that I feel like I could sooner understand the chemical composition of God.

My story is so important to me because it's the only one I have. It's as if I want to secretly own both antiquity *and* posterity, thereby skirting obsolescence altogether. I promise that one day I'll try to get over myself. But for now, please let me describe my pain to you. It hurts SO bad. Sometimes I even lock myself up in the closet of the back bedroom. At a recent job I hid in a corner to whimper. It's like I've had my morale bashed in, over and over and over and over and over again. But usually I have to eat it quietly. I just need you to know what's going on, I think because I don't want to feel like I'm all by myself in this horrible game. Where I juggle all day long and no one's giving me any pats on the back for being able to hold a simple conversation about the weather. Asking for a day pass from the bus driver is sometimes harder for me than almost anything I can think of. Like, if I jumped out of the bus as it was moving and had wings explode out of my shoulders… I think this'd be easier than having to meet the eyes of the driver. Sometimes, believe it or not, I seem perfectly normal. My neighbors see me take out the trash and they have no idea that parts are fissured inside of me, fractured, into little pieces of annihilation. When I am purchasing my toothpaste and shampoo—even though outside on my face I'm saying Thank You for giving me my pocket change—inside I'm all completely fucked up in a garbage disposal, one that smokes with a familiar silence whenever it's finished having its way with me. No matter how many rabid cats are hissing all around me, no one is hitting the pause button long enough for me to compose myself. Not even for a damn instant.

Simply put, I've worked harder at trying to function every day than most athletes do for the Olympics. From moment to moment, second to second, I have worked and worked

and worked and worked

and worked and

worked and worked and worked and worked and worked and worked and worked and worked. Every single moment. Of every single second. Of every single day. In fact, one therapist told me that I worked harder on my issues during our sessions than **any** patient he had seen in his 20-plus years of doing therapy.

I have to put most of my actions, even my thoughts, on autopilot. If I didn't have everything, and I mean pretty much everything, patternized ahead of time... I'd spin my mind into circles trying to make decisions about every little thing. What I'm about to show you elucidates the context in which my mental events occur every single moment of my life: The structure of my Constitution, a gravely intricate document which I designed myself, is inextricably bound with how I *constantly* monitor many aspects of myself. On the next page is merely the cover sheet of the Constitution, which looks maybe a little bit like extraterrestrial algorithmic code. The cover sheet is refreshed weekly. By the way, as you see all of this, never allow yourself to forget that

I stick to the Constitution *100%*

In all seriousness, I refer to the Constitution (directly or indirectly) hundreds of times within the span of one day. It's with me at all times. In addition to providing an extensive checklist of tasks which I begin the moment I wake up, the Constitution helps me with my OFF THE CHART anxiety because it allows me to channel the anxiety into organized productivity—sometimes even productivity which is specifically aimed at reducing anxiety. Part of reducing anxiety, for me, is streamlining every single aspect of my daily activities. For example, when it comes to my sleep...

~~~~~~~~~~SLEEP SYSTEM~~~~~~~~~~

__*Notes and definitions:*__

~SS is short for Sleep System.

~NAK is a combo word of Nap and Tacked On; it refers to when sleep hour requirements are not met and then are rolled over to be made up at another time. They are added to the SW.

~SW=Sleep Well; the rolled over hours make up the total of the well.

~TSW=Temporary Sleep Well.

~"Soft minimum" (SM) refers to the number of hours which constitute the rock-bottom amount that I need to reach. The "hard minimum" (HM) refers to the number of hours which, if attained during a night of sleep, creates a situation where the SW is neither added to nor subtracted from—attaining at least the HM every night is desirable. Having to add to the SW (because of not making the HM) is obviously undesirable. Conversely, being able to subtract from the SW (by surpassing the HM) is particularly desirable.

~WT=Wake-up Time; I am not allowed to wake up before or after the WT without the implementation of very simple penalties and/or, if necessary, reconfigurations of the SS for that night and the following day/night.

~LT=Lie-down Time.

~ST=Sleep Time.

~NT=Nap Time; this refers to the amount of hours that are allotted for sleep between the end of the WT and the LT.

__*Regulations:*__

I. On a standard night, my ideal target for sleep is 9-11 hours with the following stipulations:

A. WT is anywhere between 6am-10am.

B. The NT for the following day is 2 hours.

i. If I want, I can place NT directly after the close of the WT window, 10am. So, if I'm exhausted the night before and want to wake up the next day at 12pm noon, I have to deduct

the entirety of NT. For NT, LT is half an hour before actually starting the clock which measures the amount of time that will be deducted from NT.

C. The SM is 8 hours.

i. Normally, NT cannot be used to meet the SM.

ii. If the SM is not met: For every minute below the mark, the added total of these minutes is calculated to form a TSW. Special arrangements need to be made to eliminate the TSW by sleeping off these hours, preferably the same day, so that I don't have to add to the regular SW. It should go without saying that there is still time to meet the SM if the window of WT is not over. If it is, however, over... in only this case can NT be used to meet the SM. If the NT has already been exhausted in addition to the WT being over, I follow certain procedures: If the TSW amount short of the SM is not too much, say 3 hours as a rule of thumb, then I can either do some/all of these hours as extra NT; or at this point I can resort to converting the TSW time and adding it to the general SW. If, however, the TSW short of the SM is severe, say more than 3 hours, then I need to use my discretion for what's best to do... depending on my state physically/emotionally. At this point I can alter the entire SS, but I need to remember that it's important to try to do, if possible, what's also best for the more general regularity of the SS beyond the scope of just one day/night. For example, I can temporarily alter the SS by allowing myself to stretch the WT window to accommodate the needs of a particular day.

D. The HM is 9 hours.

i. If the HM is not met: For every minute below the mark, the added total of these minutes is calculated and NAK'd. I have the option of using NT to reduce the SW, if available. Though the HM is 9, I can go up to as much as I want, even 15 hours, say, but not by passing the WT window. Instead, the only way to surpass the HM is to have the LT and ST the night before set early enough to accommodate this.

a. Planning the HM and LT the night prior: Since the ideal target for sleep is 9-11 hours per night, I need to aim for an ST of 2am and an LT of 1am in order to meet the close of the WT window, the 10am deadline, AND to meet the SM. Accordingly, if I want to get 3

hours more than the HM and not use any NT to do so, I have to aim for an ST of at least 10pm and an LT of 9pm. On average, I try to make sure I am never passing an LT of 1am. (For many years it would take me 2-6 hours to fall asleep; now I use sedatives for instances of insomnia.) Finally, I aim to keep the status quo of, or reduce, the SW.

I have systems for so many activities. From oral hygiene to paper filing. The Sleep System is but one piece of my so-called Constitution. Co for short. Basically, I'm often calculating in my head. And in some of my more extreme states, I end up needing to sit aside somewhere, rocking back and forth a little bit, to tend the bonfire of my tallying. I'm also known to pace back and forth, and left to right, and back and forth, while talking to myself. I'm a state of the art computer: *if this then that, if that then this*. People often can't stand the notion of rigidly molding their every action and microthought. But for me a nightmare descends when I come across a novel situation, or one which is simply a little too outside my control. So I'd rather suffer the oppression from strict regimentation instead of the oppression from unguided moment-to-moment decision making. I have, for example, endless chains of technicalities regarding how many ounces of milk to have per day and why and under what circumstances and what kind and with what and what to use to measure it and on what countertop and up to which red notch on the beaker and how many feet away from the microwave.

I'm sure you also have to make such decisions. But the difference is that these decisions will have me gripped by the neck. They can shatter my stillness with primordial panic each and every time. Almost any variable of any activity can be the source of my mental demise. My stomach sinks and I can't breathe because I feel momentarily traumatized by the microdecision-making process. Just deciding whether to write it as microdecision versus micro-decision or versus versus vs... these decisions have the potential to cause me not only anxiety, not only discomfort, but sheer panic that makes me want to collapse to the floor and call emergency services. That's why the more I can have stuff pre-decided, the better. If not, it's throwing a monkey wrench into my hardware. I short-circuit a little.

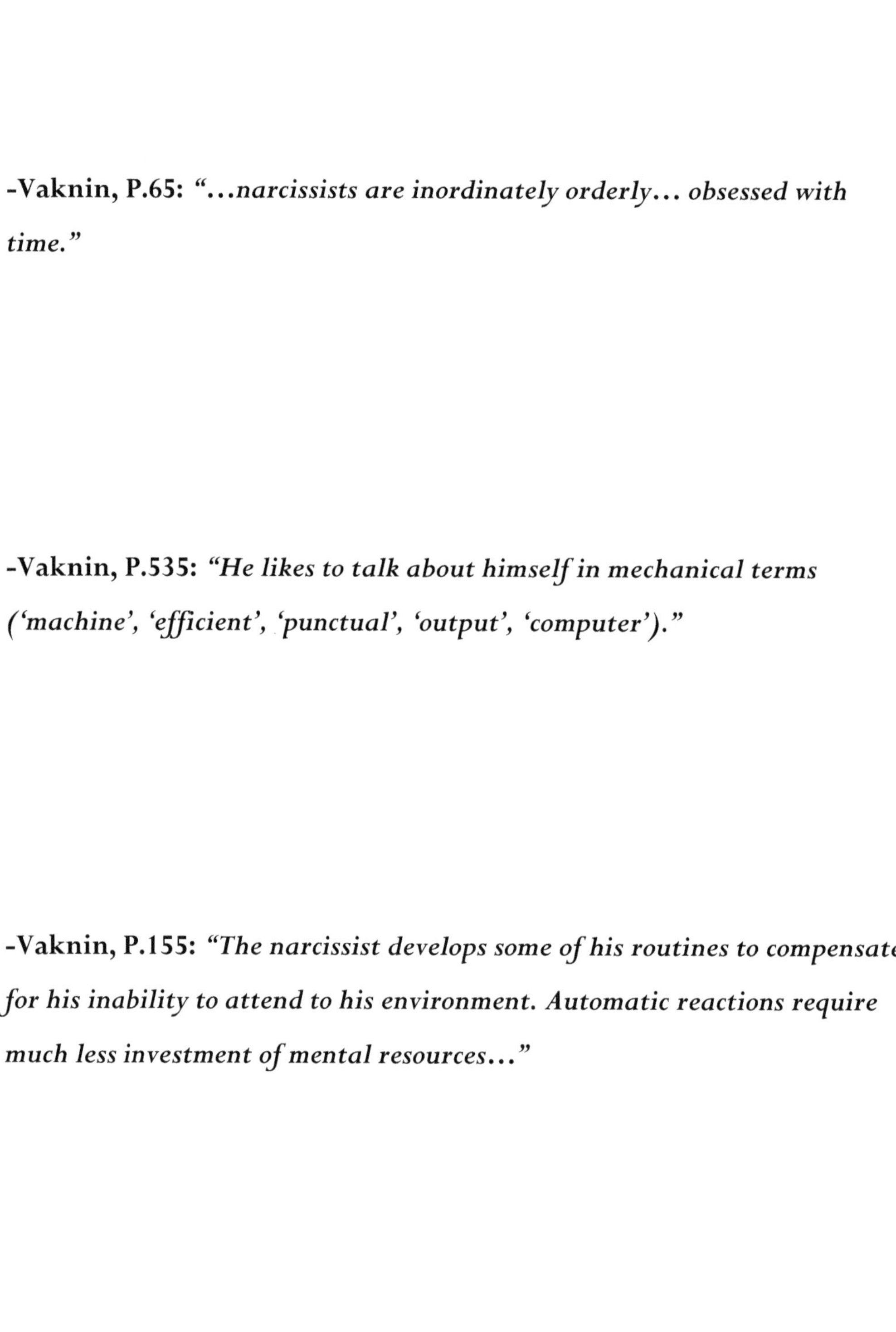

-Vaknin, P.65: *"...narcissists are inordinately orderly... obsessed with time."*

-Vaknin, P.535: *"He likes to talk about himself in mechanical terms ('machine', 'efficient', 'punctual', 'output', 'computer')."*

-Vaknin, P.155: *"The narcissist develops some of his routines to compensate for his inability to attend to his environment. Automatic reactions require much less investment of mental resources..."*

My Constitution relates to the fact that, during the earliest stages of my mental deterioration, I grew eager to become my personal best in addition to working out the kinks and knots of my psyche. I wanted to excel, become great, and attain some type of venerated noteworthiness. Enter: my obsession with self-improvement. Before I ever seriously cracked open a Self Help book, I was already making myself my own guinea pig for self-designed challenges, like making it mandatory that I drink at least 80 oz.'s of water every calendar day... or at one point aspiring to slowly integrate 777 of my favorite synonyms into my vocabulary by imposing a required review of them once a month. Many times I would be up at 4am doing push ups because I considered it nothing short of sacrilegious for me to go to sleep without having completed my Co Dailies, as I call them. Sometimes my body would even automatically start doing crunches in my sleep without me knowing it. As weird as it got, all of this was still mainly a massive project in personal betterment. I eventually learned how to better organize my priorities, to focus on achieving certain goals while still paying attention to the game of life.

So in addition to the emotional realm, the Co certainly helps me physically. I've learned, through intense discipline and through trial and error, how to shape my physique in a multitude of different ways. A huge help was *The Body Sculpting Bible for Men: The Way to Physical Perfection,* by Villepigue and Rivera. This book reminded me that, according to certain folks, it takes the average person 14 days to develop a habit (pg5). On my own, I've figured out how to get very lean to the point of scrawniness if that's the look I want, but occasionally I give slight mass to different parts of my musculature. I've even had a light six-pack. Sometimes I'm thinner, sometimes I'm average, and sometimes I'm a tad chubby on purpose. I mess with how I look. I think of myself as a shape shifter.

DIET (tailored specifically for me; not recommending that you follow this):

**** I cannot ingest the following foods under any circumstances:*** *peanut butter / ice cream / frozen yogurt / popsicles / granola bars / cereal bars / fruit n' nut bars / hamburgers / egg rolls / popcorn / chips / crackers / pretzels / pizza / all noodle and pasta products / chocolate / white bread / cheese / any drinks other than skim milk, tea, and water; carbonated non-flavored water permissible, but not flavored / all pastries, including French toast, pancakes, and waffles / all candies, excluding sugar free gum, cough drops, and medicine / (...and the list goes on)*

*** Between 8pm and 8am:** *I can only eat certain meats, certain veggies, certain fruits, and can only have certain drinks.*

**** I have two Food Vetoes:*** *which means that I can eat anything I want for a 24 hour window during 2 days each month. Regrettably, I have a habit of going outrageously food-berserk during those windows of time and end up eating so much junk food that I'll eventually find myself hunched over the toilet, throwing up.*

I cannot allow my utensils to touch restricted foods. Also, I eat very very specific portions of proteins/carbs every 2-3 hours. (My usual lunch, all mixed up together in a bowl, is as follows: peanuts, spinach, salmon, and bananas.) All provisions of the food plan are not arbitrary. Some of the bigger decisions required hours of reading, reflection, and of course, panic. I'm an utter nightmare for waitresses. But my Constitutional scheme works for me. From my last physical, I know that I'm in good health. Healthy thyroid. High rates of the good cholesterol. Low rates of the no-good. Pure liver. Highly oxygenated blood. Perfect pulse. Strong circulation. Mighty heartbeat.

Just like the American Constitution, my Co has an elaborate system through which I can make periodic "amendments" to the food plan (or any other aspect of the Co), but **only** after established waiting periods and technical due processes are met. This aspect of the Co is my saving grace, and personally I think it's clever, for it serves to lend to the Co a kind of credibility and insurance. In the primitive years of the Co, for instance, I could make amendments to it as often as I wanted. But I'd stress out about a specific policy I had in place and, due to impatient whim, I'd resolve to unnaturally expedite its modification or elimination. So essentially there was no anchor. It was just a more organized version of chaos. But now that only one amendment goes through each month, I'm forced to shut the fuck up. My relentless mental lobbyists, in other words, come to realize that it's time to pack up and go home.

What I've shown you up until now is such an itty bitty fraction of the Constitution in its grand entirety. I'll spare you the <u>pages and pages</u> of subdivisions that feed into it. The Co has countless laws, technicalities, conditions, statutes, clarifications, regulations, theories, and procedures for each and every thing. Pages and pages and pages and more, um, pages.

MADE-UP SELF HELP BOOK TITLES, AS THOUGHT OF BY ME:

~ NOT BEING ABLE TO FIND A BATHROOM AND OTHER WAYS YOUR LIFE COULD BE WORSE

~ TOTAL AND UTTER SELF-REALIZATION IN 30 MINUTES OR LESS

~ HOW TO FLY

~ SO YOU'RE HORNY AND HOPELESS?

~ STOP BITING OTHERS WHEN YOU GET ANGRY

~ 50 SUPER EXTREMELY DRAMATIC WAYS TO QUIT YOUR JOB

~ BE YOUR OWN COSMETIC SURGEON: PENIS ENLARGEMENT, BREAST IMPLANTS, AND NOSE JOBS

~ HOW TO START A GARAGE BAND WITH YOUR MOM

~ MARRYING FOR MONEY: METHODS FOR MAKING IT SEEM LIKE YOU'RE IN LOVE

~ HOW TO READ SELF HELP BOOKS WHILE DRIVING

~ TOOTHPICKS, PLUNGERS, COCKROACHES, FOIL, AND POOP: HOW ORDINARY HOUSEHOLD OBJECTS CAN SPICE UP YOUR SEX LIFE

~ GET OVER THE GUILT OF STEALING, GUARANTEED

~ CONQUERING YOUR OBSESSION WITH OTHER PEOPLE'S CHILDREN

~ GET SKINNY ENOUGH TO HIDE BETWEEN SHEETS OF PAPER

~ SPONTANEOUS HUMAN COMBUSTION, DECLARING YOURSELF PRESIDENT OF THE WORLD, FAINTING, AND OTHER STRATEGIES FOR GETTING ATTENTION

~ BECOME TOUGHER THROUGH TEAR-DUCT REMOVAL SURGERY

~ BEAT NERVOUSNESS THROUGH SWEAT-GLAND REMOVAL SURGERY

~ SELF-ESTEEM FOR LOSERS

Overall, I'd say my Constitution has definitely become more manageable nowadays compared to some of its more severe periods. During my early college years, I had bans on masturbation and certain kinds of physical contact with other people (like no kissing). At one point, I had myself watching a film every single day even if I didn't feel like it. Then there was having to read books syllable by syllable. Or making it mandatory to have weekly exercises done during specified periods—I once ended up needing to do about <u>8 hours</u> of exercise in a single day. One time I didn't eat at a Father's Day dinner with my family because it was after 10pm, and during that phase of the Co I wasn't allowed to eat anything after the 10th hour struck... my sisters were really annoyed because they simply couldn't believe that I was not willing to bend the rules just a little bit... I think it was only approximately 2 minutes after 10pm. I believe, deep in my deepest of convictions, that my Constitution would fall apart if I didn't stick to it 100%. If I allowed myself one little sip of wine just this "one time" (even though it wasn't an allotted alcohol day), or if I had a small nibble of that delish-looking tart to "live a little"... I think that the infrastructure of my reality would implode into a grizzly black hole and that I'd go even deeper into the emotional abyss and that my eyeballs would pop out and the eye cords would twist all tangled up. Okay, maybe not exactly. But I'd certainly have a severe crisis on my hands. I must stick to my Constitution with an ultra iron fist. Or it wouldn't work. I follow it religiously. Obsessively. No exceptions! None! NO NO NO.

Essentially, I use the Constitution to help me manage my own version of what is commonly known as cognitive behavioral therapy (CBT). This is a type of therapy that I do all day long, every day, to such a painstaking degree that it would blow your mind. Through diligent CBT I have modified dozens of my personal habits, both behavioral and mental. For example, to disentangle my inner dialogues revolving around anxiety, I created something I call my Panic Button. It's basically a little symbol on my hand which has countless hierarchical meanings

and, since the symbol changes every month, it is always accompanied by a different Panic Button Guide (for how to use it as a fulcrum in my own individualized CBT). I eventually made the Panic Button design permanent by having the word "RELAX!" tattooed onto my hand.

In addition to having my own cognitive programs, I've read Self Help literature dealing with different facets of anxiety. In *Don't Worry,* J. Adrienne Henderson says, "A further misunderstanding behind the idea that we control our thoughts and feelings is the assumption that our thinking is available to us. We deal only with the *end products* of the thought process, with what sticks out as novel, as a problem, after the familiar has been routinely digested" (88). In addition to the elusive quality of individual thoughts which she describes, there is their speed. In *The Anxiety Book,* Jonathan Davidson, M.D., characterizes negative thoughts "as hit-and-run fugitives: They damage your sense of security then slip away into the darkness of semi-consciousness" (90). And besides the speed of negative thoughts is their ability to occur in the present, in the form of physiologically damaging stress, even if there exists no urgent threat. In *Finding Serenity in the Age of Anxiety,* Robert Gerzon explains, "The reason is that when we obsess upon a future threat, our subconscious mind begins to perceive it as imminent and our body gets fooled into thinking it is dealing with an immediate danger" (215).

Something else that I try to apply to my own cognitive behavioral therapy is the realization that the existence of anxiety, in and of itself, is not necessarily hazardous or unhealthy. In *The Positive Power of Negative Thinking,* Julie Norem, Ph.D., talks about "rejecting the premise that feeling good should always be our most immediate aim. Empowering people to tolerate and accept negative feelings is a strength of defensive pessimism as a strategy and a capacity we may generally undervalue" (96).

Journal Entry - May 2006

Emotions:

So, for millions and gazillions of years people have been talking about love. Loneliness. Truth. I hate the fact that these words can be spoken by everyone, but that everyone isn't as much the expert as they make themselves out to be. Is it fruitless to try and brainstorm further on those themes? After all, they're the meat of every saga in theatre, of every ripe love ballad. Right now I'm listening to a song. I'm eating dinner. Feeling emotional. And I feel like, in a sense, maybe it is worth brainstorming. Either that, or lots and lots of people are wasting their time. People keep writing songs. People keep reading novels. People keep getting involved in love triangles. Sometimes I want to say GET OVER IT, humanity.

But then other times something quite ordinary will happen and I'll say OH, that's what everyone's talking about—shit—love really IS complicated. And yet here I am, thinking everyone is so gullible for feeling affected by the same old same old. But is this what we all have in common? This haunts me. Depresses me. That what I have in common with all people is that we all feel things. Sometimes very strongly. It's almost like I feel ready to evolve, to get beyond it. But the day when our species further develops the brain to the point where emotions are no longer as much a problem for us, is that the day to truly mourn? If Shakespeare and Galileo and all of the gang, as in everyone who's anyone, were to be here with me,

next to me while I type, I wonder if they'd be offended that I dare talk about these things as if I knew something. You see, it's so fucking cliché to talk about love. What more can be said? About anger? Or the human condition? But the tightness in my throat feels like it could take on an army of poets. Of aristocrats. For God's sake, please try to understand my situation: When you find yourself at the center of the entire universe, like me, you wonder why the Earth itself doesn't drop to its knees and quake each and every time you feel anything at all. Some tears just swam down my face. But there my roommate sits, just feet away from me, watching television.

I'm still eating my dinner. The whole world could flip inside out and no one would have noticed that I was just feeling so bittersweet right now. It terrifies me. Where does this emotion go? When it's all used up? It seems like there's no explanation other than it is just wasted. I think that being a social animal is just a copout for convincing ourselves that the things we are feeling somehow really matter. My tears are really coming down now. And basically, I don't know how to feel. I want to grab the world by the balls and say HEY I'm listening to a song and the words... they're moving me... HEY, I'm being moved here. I'm having a fucking moment! But something simple will slip, like I obsess about minutia, and everything distorts. I am disgusted by you and everything again. And besides, what can I say that hasn't been said? Me, a 23 year old who doesn't even make much money? Fuck. I can feel the pressure now. I don't know what to say. All I know for sure is that I wish I wasn't always so fucking distracted. I'm shaking my knees now. You know, how kids do in class when they're thinking hard.

I'm like a different kind of robot. Leaking battery acid. Perpetually. It's easy to assume that I'm bitter because I'm so unhappy. But the funny thing about being unhappy is that, from here in unhappyland, the things that can actually make people happy seem either foolish or simply

inexplicable. I am hating you and your pals and all the fun you have and all the ways that you are predictable. But... I want everyone in the world who I hate, which is pretty much everyone, to know that I really just want to be happy. That I'd be a better person if I wasn't so... I don't know... scared. If it means I have to accept all of these people, and if it means that I have to accept you, I'd like to believe that I'd do it. But that's how fucked up I am. I'm willing to hold onto my bitterness.

I have very small pockets where I feel good. Where everything is light and everything is swift. <u>Where I am fearless.</u> Those rare moments help me to feel like I love the world. But then when I start to dip, and then I dip really hard, even the incentive of feeling that good again is sometimes not enough. Maybe if I hold onto my anger, I'll be able to save it up and someday cash it in for a gold mountain of vindication. As if I had been right all along. About everything. But letting go of that, that's probably what I have to do, and so many things like that, to push myself even further toward happiness. But I'm not yet ready to be wrong. Or, not to be wrong, but to be not right. And sometimes my skin isn't even thick enough to hold up against someone giving me an ugly look. Or someone being mean to me. It crumbles me. Like the cinnamon in my plate. Fuck.

-Vaknin, P.157: ***"As 'public opinion' ebbs and flows, so do the narcissist's self-confidence, self-esteem, sense of self-worth, or, in other words, so does his Self. Even the narcissist's convictions are subject to a never-ending process of vetting by others."***

Besides anxiety, Self Help had the most jarring impact on my life when I learned about narcissism. Believe it or not, I used to be worse. (The title for this book was almost, in reference to myself: *The Most Influential Person of the 21st Century*.) Sam Vaknin's provocatively and insightfully written *Malignant Self Love* exposed me to a clinical discussion of narcissism for the first time. I initially suspected that reading about it would be helpful to my cognitive therapy, especially because I sporadically began to notice the connection between my unhappiness and my self-importance. I was unaware, however, that my pride would be in for such a trial. I learned that I am merely one narcissist amongst many, and therefore relatively unimportant. I reasoned that so many have lived, in fact, that the narcissistic archetype was able to be established in the first place. I personally think that these kinds of realizations can be psychically traumatic for a habitual narcissist. They certainly were for me. To this day I am recovering from having my very foundation ripped wide open. I am often infatuated with my newfound existential depression. Meaninglessness.

-Vaknin, P.242: ***"This is the first and, by far, the most critical step on the way to coping with the disorder: will the narcissist admit, be forced, or convinced to concede that he is absolutely and unconditionally wrong, that something is very amiss in his life, that he is in need of urgent, professional help, and that, in the absence of such help, things will only get worse?"***

^^LETTER^^ Los Angeles; March 25, 2007

Dear Reader,

I write to you at Al's request. I probably know him better than anyone, and his hope is that my written reaction to this book will add further dimension and detail to the portrait he has presented of himself. Al is perhaps the sweetest, most sensitive soul I have ever known. He also possesses startling depth and insight for someone his age, but I suspect this may be difficult to believe if your only knowledge of him comes from the book in your hands. Reading it elicited a broad range of responses from me: confusion, annoyance, shock, appreciation, awe, and finally I think, understanding.

I was almost 31 when I met Al. He was 19. I would probably never have considered talking to him again were it not for the fact that before the end of our first interaction together, Al's veneer of dried bullshit had serendipitously begun to crack and fall away. What emerged from underneath was such a vulnerable, bright, and completely endearing person. For whatever reason, I was one of the few people at the time who got to see Al's true self, and over the coming weeks I got to know and respect him. The real Al's appearances were frustratingly brief. More often I was faced with harsh Al, bitter Al, morose, self-obsessed Al. Sometimes his extreme moods and posturing just seemed to be part of that youthful, uncertain-but-grandiose phase many of us go through as we attempt to figure out who we're going to be, but in truth it was part of an intricate survival mechanism he had developed to cope with an illness and inner misery the severity of which took me years to fully comprehend. The sheer ferocity of his struggle left him constantly drained, and desperate, and angry, and heart-wrenchingly sad. Regularly he was unfriendly.

In the years since, the special and extraordinary person who came to the surface so infrequently has become more and more present, and Al's own experience of living has grown more and more positive. Though he's still a work

in progress, he now has more feelings of joy and connection to others. His transformation is truly miraculous, but a miracle of his own design and implementation. Al's recovery has been so successful thus far that upon reading this book I at first failed to recognize its pushy, self-important tone. I was confused, and more than a little put off. I found brief, fleeting moments of significance, but they were scattered and disconnected and so completely immersed in unwieldy language and pointless minutia that I was left flabbergasted. I had no idea what I was going to say to him. Salvation came only with the journal entries. To me it was like a switch was thrown and the Al that I know had reappeared. I found those pages to be wondrous for their openness and unapologetic uncertainty.

Why does he feel such an imperative need to impress people? It's when people are shown more of the real him, the damaged but hopeful him, that they become impressed and inexorably drawn to him. I've seen it happen time and again, and each time seems to surprise him. I try to explain it. He listens and understands intellectually but not in his heart, probably because his heart has suffered the most and is still healing. He is, in his true form, a broken, rebuilt, flawed, and utterly dazzling figure.

Signed, Ryan T.

•　•　•　•　•

(5 dots lined up)

For the record: Though I am mentally ill, I am not a physical threat to myself or to other people.

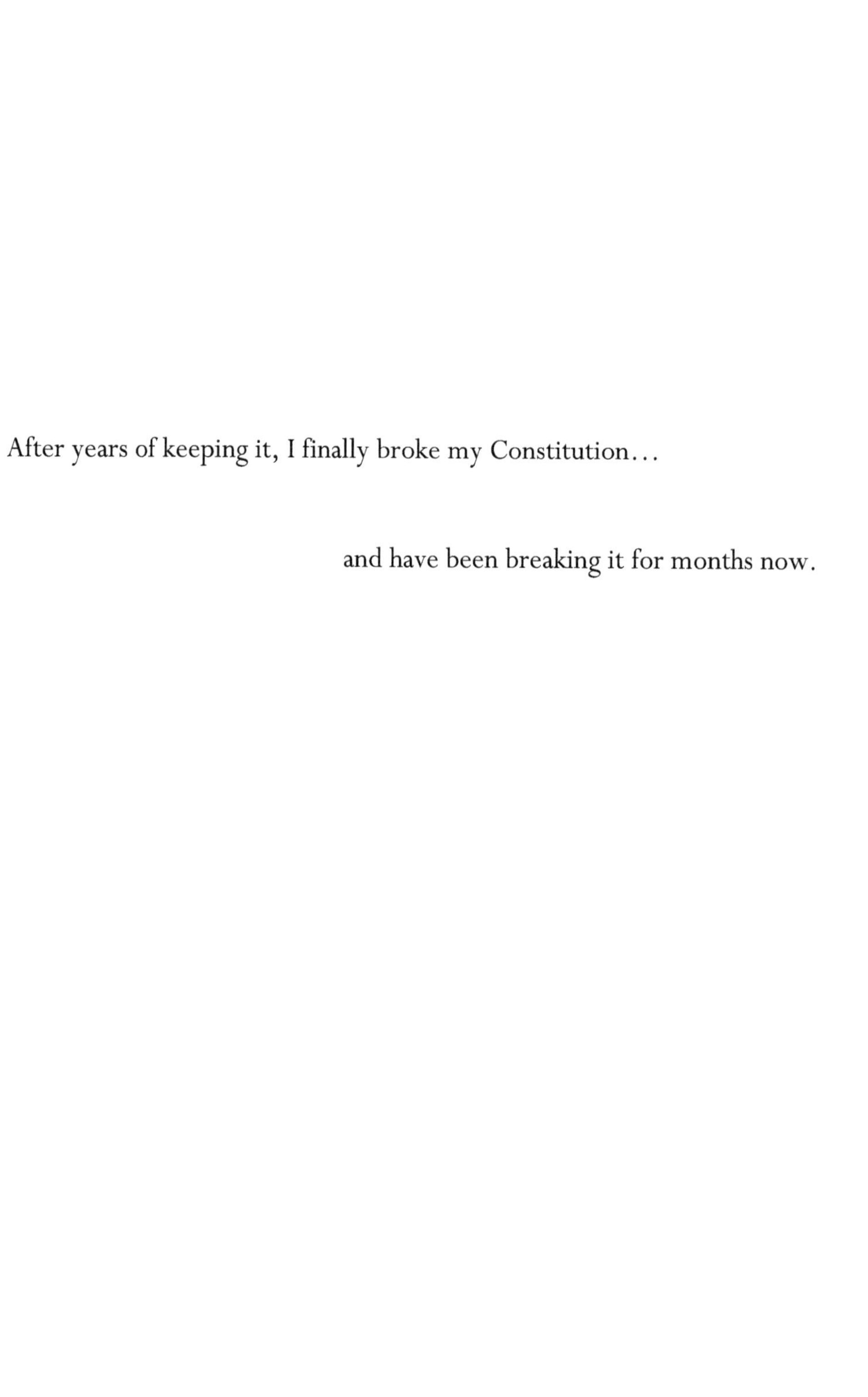

After years of keeping it, I finally broke my Constitution…

and have been breaking it for months now.

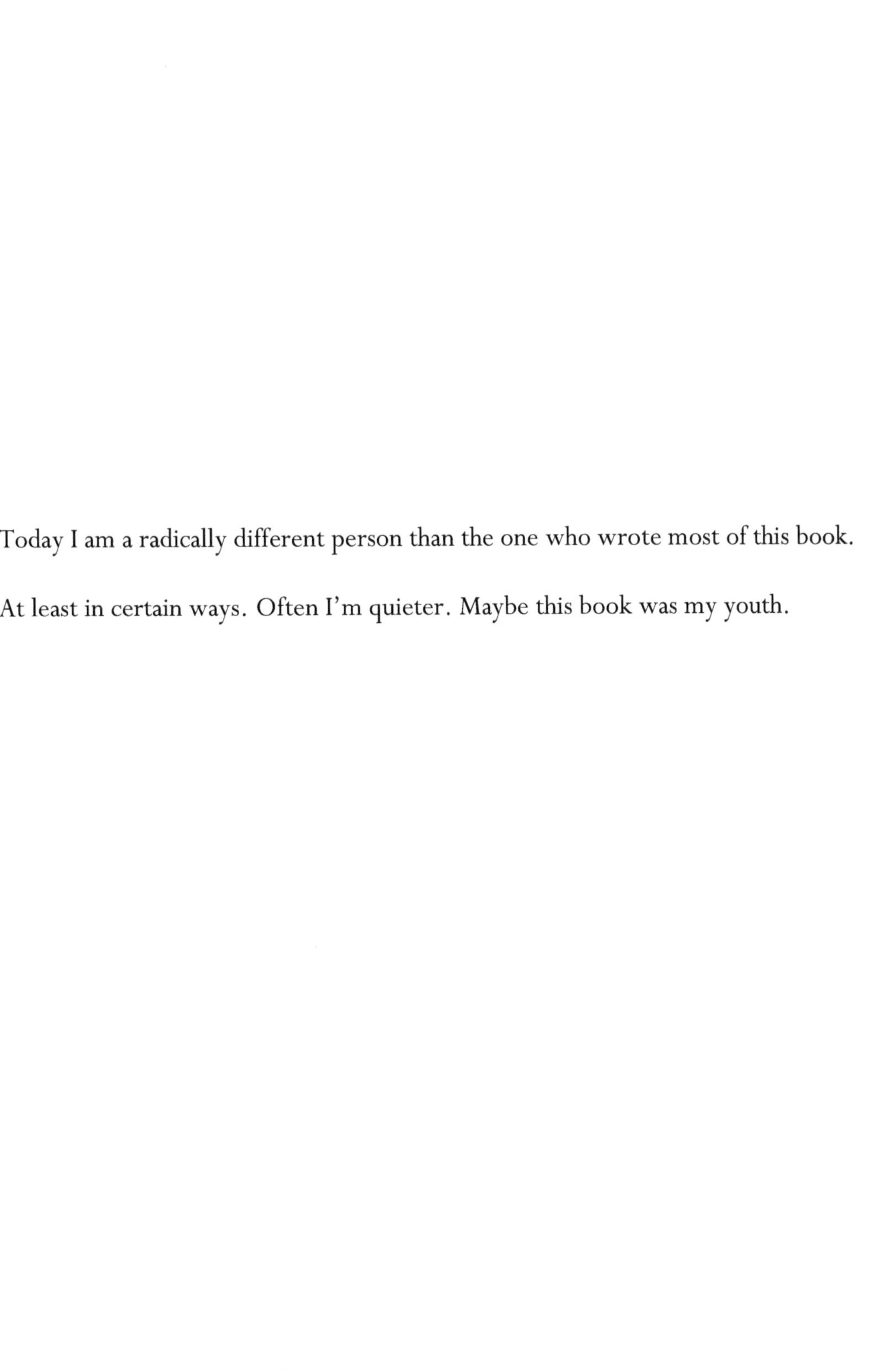

Today I am a radically different person than the one who wrote most of this book.

At least in certain ways. Often I'm quieter. Maybe this book was my youth.

I AM CLOSING MY BOOK WITH AN OLD JOURNAL PASSAGE:

UNDATED ENTRY

So I have really great news: Beauty exists in the world!!! I personally checked. It's indescribably hard for me to find it on the drop of a dime, for it's a tricky mother fucker. And yet, it exists out there. Definitely. Certainly. And this is a great relief to me; should be for you as well. Beauty is in the eye of the blah blah, yes, we know... but the important thing is that whatever form it might take for you, it's out there waiting for you. When beauty strikes me, sometimes unexpectedly, it feels almost like the planets have aligned because it's so rare... distinct to that moment in the fabric of all space and time. It's an unintelligible combination of my temperament, circumstance, the mood lingering in the air, luck, desperation, and some elusive ingredient—this is what it takes for BEAUTY itself to make its way to my forgotten neck of the woods, and for it to knock at my door. And fuck, when it knocks... it fucking knocks. It blows the door down. It lifts my feet a few inches off the ground and I swear I might even get a little lightheaded, breathing harder than usual.

That's why I think you should seek, with alarm, whatever beauty means for you. It has the power to interrupt your narrative, to yank you a little bit off center-stage like one of those big hooks that they use in cartoons to kill an act. Whatever makes the planets align for you, please find it. As often as possible. Regardless of what it takes. I think everyone needs and deserves—just for existing—adequate doses of beauty. Whether for you it's a floating plastic bag or rose petals exploding out of a cheerleader's breasts, find the fucker. And if you're one of those fellas who feels like a wuss for

trying to smell the flowers and such, goddammit, just wear a callous Anarchy t-shirt to save face. Haven't you noticed that it helps me save face in my writing by cursing when I'm doing something akin to talking about teddy bears or a song that makes me cry?

Let me tell you about things that I think are beautiful. Things that move me. I find things that are sad beautiful. So beautiful. Especially injustice. It's probably because it gives me the right to feel indignant, and therefore, it lets me fight on the side of the good. And the good, by nature, has beauty over on its side. But so does the other side. Or at least, it can. Other things that I find beautiful include when I see innocence that's not lame. Holidays? Lame. A little mouse who doesn't know what's going on in the world? Fucking beautiful. Like this one time, Ryan and I were driving at an intersection. The two of us spotted a hat across the street in the midst of traffic. We supposed that there was a tiny little mouse inside the hat who was frightened by the sound of all the cars, and that the mouse was asking out loud to the world in a confused and endearing and innocent and soft voice: "What's happening?" The idea that this little mouse didn't know WHAT was going on, but that, as Ryan and I put it, he was just "trying to be the best little mouse he could"... it fucking got to me. No, I'm not kidding. This kind of thing melts me and mushes me and makes me soft droopy clay. It makes me want to shout at the cruel skies on behalf of the little mouse. (In fact, I did shout for him. Partially because Ryan and I determined that the mouse, during his journey shortly thereafter, accidentally got squished in a mouse trap that we carelessly forgot we had left in the attic. Thinking about the mouse can make me sad to this day.)

Children's books make me cry. No joke. I mean sad ones. Bittersweet. They make me cry. They're so fucking beautiful. They make me want to go out and hug people. And to say sorry to everyone I've ever been a dick to.

Beauty can stop me dead in my tracks and put me in a state of shock quite literally. When something grabs me like that, FUUUUUUUUUUUUCK, I want it to last. The feeling. It feels so good I can barely stand it. Seriously. I can barely stand it. I need to have the right chemicals flowing through my brain. The "happy" ones like serotonin and whatnot. But it's special beyond mere biochemistry because there's also context. The beauty that I've been lucky to experience has a context, and therefore, has the effect of sometimes giving me the tiniest bit of perspective on that context. And perspective, as you might already know, is fucking beautiful.

www.alsebastiangarcia.com

APPENDIX

A brief history of American Self Help.

In order to set a basic historical/thematic context for the Self Help industry, I am going to briefly examine the influence of 13 men on the industry: Benjamin Franklin (1706-1790), Henry David Thoreau (1817-1862), Ralph Waldo Emerson (1803-1882), William James (1842-1910), Sigmund Freud (1856-1939), Dale Carnegie (1888-1955), Norman Vincent Peale (1898-1993), Abraham Maslow (1908-1970), Carl Rogers (1902-1987), Stephen Covey (born 1932), Anthony Robbins (born 1960), Phillip McGraw (born 1950), and Deepak Chopra (born 1946). This grouping was reached after careful consideration, and it is by no means exhaustive. Also, every member of the group is not necessarily self-identified as a Self Help writer. There are, however, commonalities amongst the 13. Many of them hold records (such as book sales, internet searches, television ratings) that have dwarfed those of nearly all other Self Help writers to date. Many of them are or have been worldwide speakers, seminar leaders, and the heads of highly successful companies/organizations. Regardless of their similarities, this list is obviously just one of many possible combinations that could guide a discussion on Self Help. Excluded are countless nutritionists, theorists, women, etc.[ii]

Though Benjamin Franklin, of the 18th Century United States, was one of the very last writers I was exposed to in my Self Help research, there are various reasons to unpack his work before the other 12. First, he is ahead of the others chronologically. This conveniently marks the beginning of a timeline that will allow for sequential discussions of each author within the social context of his own time. Secondly, due to the fact that Franklin's work flourished the earliest, it was able to influence some of the very authors making up the list of 13. I often feel that Franklin was unique in his commitment to Self Help during the time that he was alive, but of course such a claim is confined to the realm of opinion. In *American Philanthropy,* Robert H. Bremner declares that the Massachusetts politician and pioneer, Horace Mann, "had been a poor boy who studiously observed the maxims of self-help in his own career, and he preached those maxims with less humor and even more zeal than Benjamin Franklin" (68).

Though Franklin's level of commitment is negotiable, it stands all the same that both his personal approach and style of presentation were unique given his (1) bitter socioeconomic origins and (2) American colonial environment. Steven Starker (the author of *Oracle at the Supermarket*)—along with other evaluators of the industry—considers the roots of Self Help as belonging to a Protestant New England in which Puritan leaders delivered prescriptive guidelines, specifically for how to integrate personal lifestyle with religious observation.[iii] Starker frames Franklin's work as a token of the growing secularization which drew away from

late 17th/early 18th Century works like Cotton Mather's *Bonifacius: Essays to Do Good.* Starker says, "Where his seventeenth century Puritan predecessors had envisioned people performing their good works within the confines of well-established social roles, and thought personal ambition a sin, Franklin's writing encouraged attempts to rise in the social hierarchy by one's own efforts" (14). Though Starker believes that the Puritan ethic was colossal in its infusion of values (like diligence and thrift) into Self Help literature for decades to come, he recognizes that authors such as Franklin helped to popularize the Self Help book as a repository of practical knowledge in addition to its original use as moral guide.

One example of this is Franklin's possible influence on contemporary educational theories. Dale Schunk and Barry Zimmerman are the editors of *Self-Regulation of Learning and Performance: Issues and Educational Applications.* In this book, Zimmerman has a piece entitled, "Dimensions of Academic Self-Regulation: A Conceptual Framework for Education," in which he describes how Franklin, in his *Autobiography,* mastered "the art of formal writing through modeling. When he came upon a written passage that was especially well written, he would try to emulate it" (3). Furthermore, Zimmerman follows his mention of Franklin by highlighting the parallel, contemporary use of audio tape and video for skill learning, writing exercises, and even self-relaxation. Besides trying to be a master of his own learning, often encouraging people to read widely, Franklin also attempted methods for self-control. Butler-Bowdon (author of *50 Self-Help Classics*) says, "The famous example of Franklin's self-help ethic is what has become known as *The Art of Virtue,* in which he listed the 12 qualities he aimed to possess. By a system of graphs and daily self-appraisal, he claimed to have (mostly) achieved the desired virtues…" (147).

Franklin had various involved pursuits, one of which was his yearly series called *Poor Richard's Almanack.* In a 2004 reissue of Franklin's line of almanacs, Andrew S. Trees writes the overall Introduction. In it, he describes Franklin's story as, amongst other things, a classic rags to riches story that inspires emulation in others. Trees quotes Franklin (speaking as Poor Richard Saunders) to show that Franklin readily admitted his lack of money: "'The plain truth of the matter is, I am excessively poor, and my wife, good woman, is, I tell her, excessive proud.' With that introduction, Poor Richard had established himself as a man much like his almanac readers, an adept common touch that was always a hallmark of Franklin's writing" (ix). Other characteristics kept Franklin's series in such strong circulation that it was able to obtain lasting posterity. In *Benjamin Franklin: An American Life,* Walter Isaacson explains that Franklin had innovative marketing techniques, such as using elaborate hoaxes to garner interest. Isaacson also notes Franklin's ability for rewording common sayings in a fashion more pithy. Isaacson considers this one of the most memorable aspects of Franklin's work, saying, "Poor Richard's delightful annual prefaces never, alas, became as famous as the maxims and sayings that Franklin scattered in the margins of his almanacs each

year, such as the most famous of all: 'Early to bed and early to rise, makes a man healthy, wealthy and wise.' Franklin would have been amused by how faithfully these were praised by subsequent advocates of self-improvement..." (98).

Henry David Thoreau and Ralph Waldo Emerson, two token Transcendentalists of the 19th Century, are both examples of other early writers who have inspired values in contemporary self-improvement. In *The Essential Transcendentalists,* Richard Geldard explains that the Transcendentalist movement aimed for a combination of science, religion, and literature that rose above material reality and the human senses. He says, "It was the ambition of the Transcendentalists in New England to create a coherent and unified vision that would eventually include elements of early Christianity, Greek Philosophy, natural science, and artistic imagination" (6). In *Natural Life: Thoreau's Worldly Transcendentalism,* David Robinson further characterizes Transcendentalists as people who were interested in leading lives of simplicity. Of Thoreau's essays *WALKING* and *Life Without Principle,* he says, "These essays, whose central purpose is to serve as a guidebook for conducting a natural life, provide the context for Thoreau's later work both as a naturalist and as an engaged political critic" (162).

Thoreau is characterized as a political critic, partially because some of his personal actions and beliefs were seen as comments on how to reshape society; one example was his distaste for the slavery to which he was exposed. As a Transcendentalist, he considered socially conscious behavior to be reflected not only by public policy, but also by private matters such as the proper cultivation of friendship. Robinson says, "Remaking and revitalizing the concept and practice of friendship was a fundamental concern of the Transcendentalists, and discussions of the workings of human relationships were very much in the air in the late 1830's and early 1840's" (64). This is interesting because, coincidentally, Thoreau and Emerson developed a friendship of their own; their speculations on the idea of friendship, therefore, lent their own relationship a special importance that would inevitably affect their work. Robinson says:

> As their relationship grew, and strains became more and more prominent, Thoreau developed his own distinctive approach to the set of intellectual issues that Emerson had addressed in his early works. But Thoreau's first response, one that seems to have been operative for the most part through the writing of *Walden,* was to extend Emerson's viewpoint radically, turning Emerson's own words against him. Emerson preached the spiritual value of nature, and Thoreau became a dedicated naturalist; Emerson preached non-conformity and self-reliance, and Thoreau refused any ordinary professional path and went to live in the woods. Emerson preached an austere, rigorously demanding, and essentially self-denying form of friendship, and Thoreau echoed his

sentiments in thunder, even while he craved Emerson's acceptance, support, and intellectual guidance (71).

Steven Starker says that the New Thought movement was in certain respects anti-materialistic because of the earlier ideas of Thoreau and Emerson. Furthermore, Starker explains that the Self Help tradition changed in the latter part of 19th Century to accommodate an America that was increasingly scientific, urban, and industrial. In explaining an aspect of New Thought, he says, "This philosophy appeared as a popular religious movement that transcended the traditional denominations and included among its membership such groups as: Harmony, Unity, Mental Science, Metaphysical Healing, Divine Science, Church of Religious Science, and others" (20).[iv] Starker claims that William James was one of the few mainstream academic voices supporting New Thought. In fact, James' *The Varieties of Religious Experience* mentions mystical experiences and altered states of consciousness. Starker says, "While he did not offer any simple, popularized explanation for such phenomena, he made it clear that established philosophies could not explain all of human experience and invited a serious exploration of inner life" (23).

For James, part of the exploration of inner life was a consideration of habit formation. In *Psychology: The Briefer Course,* he declares that "we must make automatic and habitual, as early as possible, as many useful actions as we can…" (11). In this same text, he also espouses certain educational guidelines, much like Benjamin Franklin had done. For example, James says that the same materials "taken in gradually, day after day, recurring in different contexts, considered in various relations, associated with other external incidents, and repeatedly reflected on, grow into such a system, form such connections with the rest of the mind's fabric, lie open to so many paths of approach, that they remain permanent possessions" (163). In another part of the text, James explores issues regarding the human senses, a topic that was engaged often by the Transcendentalists. He explains that the phrase "'practice makes perfect' is notorious in the field of motor accomplishments. But motor accomplishments depend in part on sensory discrimination" (119). In *Pragmatism: A New Name for Some Old Ways of Thinking,* James' discussion of the senses is more geared toward issues about belief. James had a "cash value" for beliefs, and its essence is summarized by him in *Pragmatism* when he says, "The practical value of true ideas is thus primarily derived from the practical importance of their objects to us" (104).

Sigmund Freud, whose life straddled both the 19th and 20th Century, is an early example in addition to James of Self Help's relationship to the field of Psychology. In *Freud: The Mind of the Moralist,* Philip Rieff discusses the cultural significance of Freudianism and the rise of the psychoanalytic method. Rieff—who considers Western culture responsible for producing egoists concerned with their own emotions—explains, "A new discipline was needed to fit this introversion of

interest, and Freudian psychology, with its ingenious interpretations of politics, religion, and culture in terms of the inner life of the individual and his immediate family experiences, exactly filled the bill" (5). Though Rieff highlights the fact that Freud considered his own approach as method and not doctrine, he also describes how Freud combined strict medical judgments with contemporary moral critiques.

Rieff also considers Freud's reaction to Romanticism, explaining that what the Romantics had seen as a vice of reason, namely its ability to retard spontaneity, Freud saw as beneficial to his own methods. Rieff says, "Simply by the act of being brought to consciousness, Freud presumes, the spontaneity of desire will be weakened. On just this Romantic pessimism Freud based the curative hope of his therapy" (93). The Freudian therapy style is concerned with the inner life of the patient, much like in the work of William James. One idea, for example, that Freud himself employed was the notion of psychic freedom. Freedom, he believed, was a metaphor for an inner event which could be utilized anywhere, regardless of politics or the pressure of social conformity. Rieff says, "Thus Freud undermined the ancient concern of political philosophy and substituted for it the inquiry of a political psychology, asking in what manner and degree must the individual be constrained within his social relations" (256). Freud believed that certain personal constraints could be mitigated by training oneself to expect disappointment. Rieff confirms this when he explains that a "subtle acceptance of things as they are which changes the very condition to which one is resigned becomes the aim of Freudianism" (327).

Rieff notes that for Freud, this type of realistic thinking also meant having realistic expectations of therapy. Specifically, Rieff says, Freud believed that by acknowledging a pervasive and common unhappiness in life conditions, one could learn to avoid damaging pleasures while simultaneously seeing psychoanalysis as an aid in personal management (in lieu of full cure). In addition to the analyses of patients, Freud participated in a Self Help tradition of self-analysis. In *Reading Freud: A Chronological Exploration of Freud's Writings,* Jean-Michel Quinodoz says of Freud, "He thus began to make a systematic analysis of his own parapraxes – forgetfulness and slips of the tongue – just as he had analyzed his own dreams" (46).

Dale Carnegie, whose career took off in the early 20th Century, is the next person to be considered in this historical outline. His work shows instances of influence from the psychologists previously discussed. For example, in *The Giants of Sales,* Tom Sant explains, "The nineteenth-century psychologist, William James, who is often cited by Dale Carnegie, argued that the process of transforming the booming, buzzing confusion of sensory stimuli that surrounds us when we are infants into a comprehensible understanding of the world is a process of creating mental maps of the relationships among bits of our experience" (156). This relates to Carnegie's interest in neurolinguistic programming, or NLP, which Butler-

Bowdon explains was "pioneered by John Grinder and Richard Bandler and arose out of the study of how language, verbal and non-verbal, can affect the nervous system" (253). Besides NLP's conception of how we use filters and maps to interpret reality, especially with regard to what it allows us to generalize about behavior, Sant says that Carnegie was interested in NLP as a way to know how people habitually process information. (Such knowledge, Carnegie believed, might allow for the modification of how others think.)

Besides being influenced by different facets of Psychology, Sant says that Carnegie himself "discovered truths about human relationships that have been used by such powerhouse business leaders as Lee Iacocca, Mary Kay Ash, and Tom Monahan to build businesses" (3). These so-called truths had as their foundation a thorough evaluation of customer needs, which for Carnegie not only consisted of customer expectations for traditional perks such as comfort, but also their desire to feel good about themselves. Sant says that for "Carnegie, the most fundamental 'want' of all was to be valued, to feel important" (99). To this day, Carnegie's company teaches these kinds of lessons to its students. Initially a lecturer on public speaking skills, Carnegie's eventual success is noteworthy, Sant says, because Carnegie "wasn't the first to write a self-improvement book, but he was one of the first to get rich from it. His success has inspired hundreds of others" (112).

Carnegie's life is a tale of rags to riches just as in the case of Benjamin Franklin. Coincidentally, Franklin's influence on Carnegie is conspicuous. In *How to Win Friends and Influence People,* Carnegie emphasizes the importance of breaking the personal habit of being argumentative. As a good model for this he points to Franklin, saying, for "improving your personality, read Benjamin Franklin's autobiography—one of the most fascinating life stories ever written, one of the classics of American literature" (121). In another part of his book, he explains, "Benjamin Franklin, tactless in his youth, became so diplomatic, so adroit at handling people, that he was made American Ambassador to France" (13).

Carnegie's *How to Stop Worrying and Start Living* elucidates yet another instance where his business methods were influenced by thinkers already discussed in this historical outline. Regarding lessons of simplicity and cost, Carnegie mentions that "Henry Thoreau dipped his goose quill into his homemade ink and wrote in his diary: 'The cost of a thing is the amount of what I call life, which is required to be exchanged for it immediately or in the long run.' To put it another way: we are fools when we overpay for a thing in terms of what it takes out of our very existence" (84). While extrapolating upon his interpretation of Thoreau's statement, Carnegie gives a real life case of two musicians who, in his opinion, exemplified the lack of attention to cost. He considers them unfortunate because, though the duo produced great music together, their personal squabbles regarding their musical endeavors—which included trivial matters like the cost of theater carpet—ultimately, in Carnegie's eyes, negated the value of their art.

Norman Vincent Peale's most widely read work, *The Power of Positive Thinking,* was originally published in the 1950's. It shows instances of how Peale was influenced by the field of Psychology, as Carnegie had been. In line with other Self Help authors' emphasis on talk therapy and self-examination, Peale says, "Get a competent counselor to help you understand why you do what you do. Learn the origin of your inferiority and self-doubt feelings which often begin in childhood. Self-knowledge leads to a cure" (13). Earlier, I discussed Freud's idea of "common unhappiness." Peale also delivered suggestions for how to manipulate one's own interpretation to trying situations. In *You Can If You Think You Can,* Peale insists that in order for a person to be able to diffuse the threat of outside circumstances, "He must have the insight to perceive the inner cause of his defeat" (9). In *The Power of Positive Thinking,* Peale shares with Carnegie and others an emphasis on ridding worry. He describes a type of visualization exercise, saying, "This process of mind drainage is important in overcoming worry, for fear thoughts, unless drained off, can clog the mind and impede the flow of mental and spiritual power" (117).

Peale, in certain ways considered an inspiration for the Human Potential Movement, is listed in this Self Help timeline for various reasons. His work reflects the emphasis of many contemporary Self Help authors on self-esteem, motivation, success, and everyday problems. Richard Weiss, author of *The American Myth of Success: From Horatio Alger to Norman Vincent Peale,* goes as far as saying, "As a popularizer of the mentalistic self-help tradition, Peale is without peer, past or present. He markets his inspiration with all the flair of a top-notch entrepreneur" (224). For Weiss, Peale was unique in his time because he repackaged Christianity as scientific and modern to a huge popular audience, selling these ideas the way an adept businessman might.[v] Another populist aspect of Peale's work is its anti-intellectualistic slant. Weiss explains that Peale considered academic success unimportant, saying, "This reflects the democratic quality of his appeal, which is directed to ordinary people and pays homage to the common sense of 'plain folk'" (225).

A focus on the inner experience of thought and emotion, discussed by Peale and others thus far, is reflected in the Humanistic Psychology movement as initiated by Abraham Maslow and others in the 1950's. Maslow's Humanistic approaches, which differed from the traditions of Behaviorism and Freudianism, included theories about the stages of self-actualization.[vi] Furthermore, Maslow considered these stages hierarchically in terms of need, with self-actualization itself being the greatest need of the human being. In *Toward a Psychology of Being,* Maslow says that an empirical and theoretical "case has been made for the presence within the human being of a tendency toward, or need for growing in a direction that can be summarized in general as self-actualization…" (171). For Maslow, the idea of general self-actualization included sub-facets like unity of personality, creativity, and healthy identity, which in turn could provide for esteemed values like courage

and selflessness. Sant, the author of *The Giants of Sales,* sees Carnegie's conception of human needs as influencing Maslow. He explains that even though Maslow's major work came more than two decades after Carnegie's *How to Win Friends and Influence People,* both "authors recognized that in modern society, most people have little problem getting their physiological and safety needs met, and thus they don't think about those needs much" (101).

That may sound like an oversimplification, but it is a conceptualization of just one aspect of Maslow's research, which in actuality was approached sophisticatedly. In a side-bar comment provided by the editors of a 1998 reissue of *Maslow on Management,* it says, "He did not spew forth this new approach in psychology without much thought, rigorous testing, hypothesizing and debate. Thus, his work has powerfully affected managerial theory, organizational development, education, health care, and science as well as psychology" (3). Maslow considered his own work as a reaction to Freud. In *Toward a Psychology of Being,* he says it's as if "Freud supplied to us the sick half of psychology and we must now fill it out with the healthy half" (7). For Maslow, Freud's focus on pathology irrevocably prevented patients from becoming aware of their own potential. Maslow considered talk therapy a viable option for growth—much like Peale had advised readers to "get a competent counselor"—but Maslow ultimately believed that many life challenges could be solved by turning inward, without outside aid. This, he believed, was especially important to remember during the later stages of growth, which, in his opinion, required people to rely more on themselves than on others. In *Toward a Psychology of Being,* he says, "Even in principle, many of the tasks of self-actualization are largely intrapersonal, such as the making of plans, the discovery of self, the selection of potentialities to develop, the construction of a life-outlook" (43).

Carl Rogers, another key developer of Humanistic Psychology, shared certain aspects of Maslow's respect for individualism. In the Introduction to a 1995 reissue of Rogers' *On Becoming a Person: A Therapist's View of Psychotherapy,* Peter Kramer says, "Despite its origins in the helping relationship, Rogers's philosophy is grounded in Thoreau and Emerson, in the primacy of self-reliance" (xiv). Kramer describes Rogers as the foremost researcher and psychologist during the United States in the 1960's[vii], saying, "From Rogers comes our contemporary emphasis on self-esteem and its power to mobilize a person's other strengths. Rogers's understanding of acceptance as the ultimate force implies that people who are not ill can benefit from therapy and that nonprofessionals can act as therapists…" (x).

Rogers, like Maslow, is partially characterized as a reactionary against Freud. For Rogers, the "acceptance as the ultimate force" which Kramer refers to, specifically pertained to the conception of a new client-based psychotherapeutic model (where the patient could experience unconditional positive regard from the practitioner). Kramer contrasts this to Freud's approach, which he says saw the

procurement of treatment as arising from a process that set out to frustrate the patient. Freud, Kramer explains, considered anxiety in patients to be a necessary component in their being able to accept truths about themselves, as explicated by the practitioner. Rogers fundamentally disagreed with this principle, and instead believed that guidance worked best when it put faith in the decision-making abilities of the patient. In *A Way of Being,* Rogers says, "The individual in this nurturing climate is free to choose *any* direction, but actually selects positive and constructive ways. The actualizing tendency is operative in the human being" (134).

Rogers' *A Way of Being* traces his personal and professional development throughout his lifetime. It is particularly insightful into the nature of his work because, written in the early 1980's[viii], it comes toward the end of his career. Furthermore, it concludes with a series of his own optimistic predictions regarding the direction of Psychology. For example, at one point he says, "There is a new realization that the person is a *process,* rather than a fixed set of habits. This evokes altered ways of behaving, increases the options" (346). This interest in new models for describing patients further reinforces Rogers' ties to Maslow. For Maslow, self-actualizing individuals possessed an openness to both inner and outer experience. Similarly, Rogers believed that openness to experience could act as a foundation for different forms of acceptance. In his *On Becoming a Person,* Rogers says, "As a client moves toward being able to accept his own experience, he also moves toward the acceptance of the experience of others" (174).

There remain 4 men to be discussed in this timeline, and unlike those already mentioned, the remaining ones are all still currently alive. First is Stephen Covey. For Covey, the idea of accepting oneself and others (as espoused by Rogers) also entails having an attitude of win/win, where any success afforded to the individual isn't at the expense of another. Butler-Bowdon explains, "Having studied the success literature of the last 200 years for a doctoral dissertation, Covey was able to draw a distinction between what he termed the 'personality ethic'—the quick-fix solutions and human relations techniques that had pervaded much of the writing in the twentieth century—and the 'character ethic'—which revolved around unchanging personal principles" (97). It is this character ethic which Covey sets out to restore, of which, Butler-Bowdon says, Covey considers Benjamin Franklin a prime example. In his *Seven Habits of Highly Effective People: Powerful Lessons in Personal Change,* Covey traces the initial shift between the two "ethic" approaches. He explains that shortly after "World War I the basic view of success shifted from the Character Ethic to what we might call the *Personality Ethic,* success became more a function of personality, of public image, of attitudes and behaviors, skills and techniques, that lubricate the processes of human interaction" (19).

Covey's *Seven Habits,* which came out in the 1990's[ix], quickly attained the kind of sales records that took Carnegie at least 60 years to match with his *How to*

Win Friends and Influence People. In his book, Covey espouses habits like being proactive. Furthermore, he suggests that we should examine our interpretations of life events, much like some of the other authors earlier mentioned. Covey says, "The more aware we are of our basic paradigms, maps, or assumptions, and the extent to which we have been influenced by our experience, the more we can take responsibility for those paradigms..." (29). Covey's emphasis on examining how we react to situations is again seen in *Principle Centered Leadership,* where he says, "So on the continuum you go from being a victim to self-determining creative power through self-awareness of the power to choose your response to any condition or conditioning" (42).

Covey at times gives concrete suggestions in his *Seven Habits,* such as the idea of having a personal mission statement. Even though Covey believes that the content and form of each personal mission statement will vary, reflecting the uniqueness of each person, his basic premise for the mission statement is coincidentally introduced in a manner nearly identical to my own original Constitution. In the main part of this book I describe my Constitution, a personal contract of regimentation and regulation, by briefly comparing it to the structure of the American Constitution. Similarly, Covey says that the personal mission statement can be thought of as a Constitution, and even compares it to the American one. Covey believes that the structure of a public Constitution, such as the American one, can be retranslated so that it "becomes a personal constitution, the basis for making major, life-directing decisions, the basis for making daily decisions in the midst of the circumstances and emotions that affect our lives" (108). This type of personal contract is reminiscent of Covey's suggestions elsewhere to adopt business models for the personal arena. Even his son, Stephen M. R. Covey, is inspired to explore these kinds of business models in his own book, *The SPEED of Trust: The One Thing that Changes Everything.* In the Foreword of the book, Covey senior highlights the connection between personal character and business when he stresses the ties of "ethical character, transparent motivation, and superb competence in producing sustained, superior results" (xxiv).

Anthony Robbins, yet another rags to riches story, also exploded onto the Self Help scene in the 1990's. Butler-Bowdon describes Robbins as an American household name who embodies the image of the personal transformation guru. Butler-Bowdon says, "Other self-help titans like Deepak Chopra and Wayne Dyer are low key in comparison. Lots of people are willing to pay over $1,000 to attend a Robbins weekend seminar..." (253). Robbins is again another author of this timeline who cites Benjamin Franklin as a personal influence. In *Unlimited Power: The New Science of Personal Achievement,* Robbins suggests that the reader look into Franklin's *Autobiography* for tips on how to build audience rapport as an effective communicator. Robbins says, "Old Ben Franklin knew how to persuade by being certain not to create any resistance to his proposals through the use of words that trigger negative responses" (279).

In addition to being influenced by Franklin, Robbins also shares with many of the previous authors an interest in managing internal, emotional reactions to outside circumstances. In *Awaken the Giant Within: How to Take Immediate Control of Your Mental, Emotional, Physical, and Financial Destiny!,* Robbins says, "Too many of us leave ourselves at the mercy of outside events over which we may have no control, failing to take charge of our emotions—over which we have *all* the control and relying instead on short-term quick fixes" (26). Robbins' ideas on emotional mastery are heavily influenced by habit-formation theories and NLP, just as in the case of Carnegie. In a different portion of *Awaken the Giant Within,* Robbins says, "Begin today to develop the habit of focusing on the consequences of all your beliefs" (98). Additionally, in *Giant Steps: Small Changes to Make a Big Difference,* he says, "Any pattern of thinking, feeling, or behavior that is consistently reinforced will become a habit" (166).

Managing internal, emotional reactions to outside circumstances is spun differently in the work of Phillip McGraw, known to many simply as "Dr. Phil." McGraw considers Psychology, as it is now practiced, as being too ambiguous and abstract. In *Life Strategies: Doing What Works, Doing What Matters,* McGraw says, "You don't just need insight and understanding into your problems; you need them to change, right now" (23). His imperative tone is reflected in everything he writes, and according to Sophia Dembling and Lisa Gutierrez—authors of *The Making of Dr. Phil: The Straight-Talking True Story of Everyone's Favorite Therapist*—this style is perfect for the medium of television because it gets to the point quickly. The two authors describe how McGraw went from first appearing on the *Oprah Winfrey Show* in 1998, to eventually becoming, in their assessment, the most famous pop psychologist in 21st Century America. The level of frankness in his in-your-face style, which consists of catch phrases like "GET REAL," has even made guests cry. Of this, Dembling and Gutierrez say, "With his no-bull message and take-no-prisoners style, McGraw has tapped directly into the anxious zeitgeist of the time, creating the perfect character in the down-home doc who stands ready to clean up our act without taking any guff" (241).

And yet, though he engages in such a stern approach, he emulates Franklin's and Carnegie's tradition of emphasizing how we treat the people with whom we interact. In his *Life Strategies,* McGraw says, "To manage people effectively, you must do it in a way that protects or enhances their self-esteem" (49). In *Relationship Rescue,* McGraw explains that the quality of our interactions with others is ultimately sourced in the work we do on ourselves. He says, "Propel yourself to deal with the truth about yourself, even if it hurts. Prepare your heart and mind to be open rather than defensive. It is cowardly to blame, and it is cowardly and self-destructive to be in denial" (35). McGraw also speaks out against blaming others in *The Self Matters Companion: Helping You Create Your Life from the Inside Out.* He says, "As always, your ability to understand and tune into

your authentic self depends on your willingness to get real about where you are right now and how you got there" (134).

Attempts at better knowing oneself are also espoused by Deepak Chopra. In *Ageless Body, Timeless Mind: The Quantum Alternative to Growing Old,* he says, "Self-knowledge is an anchor that makes unpredictability tolerable" (178). Also, just like many of the authors already discussed, Chopra's work touches on the management of internal, emotional reactions to outside circumstances. In another portion of *Ageless Body,* Chopra says, "When you begin to get into the habit of consciously and carefully examining your old interpretations in this way, you create a space for spontaneous moments of freedom" (180). Though certain aspects of Chopra's influence started slightly earlier than that of McGraw or Robbins, he is presented last in this timeline because, unlike the other 12, Chopra is a prime popularizer of Eastern Philosophy to the American masses.[x] His emphasis is on the mind-body aspects of *Ayurveda,* the Hindu healing philosophy. He even makes dietary suggestions based on Eastern practices, explaining in *Ageless Body* that in India, "longevity was traditionally assigned to a branch of learning called *Ayurveda,* derived from two Sanskrit roots, *Ayus,* or 'life,' and *Veda,* meaning 'science' or 'knowledge'" (269). Certain facets of Eastern thought also manifest in Chopra's interest in alternative medicine. In a book review in *The Permanente Journal,* Charles Elder, M.D., says, "One bestselling author of medical self-help guides is Deepak Chopra, MD, who for 15 years has written prolifically on behalf of the holistic care movement" (11).

Chopra's implementation of Eastern traditions also extends to using meditative approaches. In *The Path to Love: Spiritual Strategies for Healing,* Chopra discusses stillness as a form of ecstasy. He says, "This process of shifting from activity to stillness is a simple yet very deep description of meditation" (290). Regardless of his respect for tradition, Chopra's popularization of Eastern thought in the United States is unique because Chopra does not fully condemn the desire for material wealth—in his view, it is not always unhealthy or necessarily out of touch with spiritual growth. Instead, he believes that wealth is in tandem with the universe because we are all economic actors subject to the realities of a modern economy. In *Creating Affluence: The A-to-Z Steps to a Richer Life,* he says, "Affluence is the experience in which our needs are easily met and our desires spontaneously fulfilled. We feel joy, health, happiness, and vitality in every moment of our existence" (21).

Regarding Self Help groups.

Certain authors believe that the modern Self Help group—in which therapy is at times performed by nonprofessionals—derives directly from the Human Potential Movement. Alcoholics Anonymous is a widely recognized example of this group model. In *The Real AA: Behind the Myth of 12-Step Recovery,* Ken Ragge frames the humble beginnings of the organization when he says, "In 1939, shortly after its founding, Alcoholics Anonymous was in debt and its membership broke. Hope for the organization's financial stability was pinned to the sale of their newly published book; *Alcoholics Anonymous*" (1). Ragge goes on to explain that a new member came up with an idea to help book sales: He'd use his connections to get a radio broadcast, and then he'd be able to plug how the AA group helped him become sober. Only the rest of the members knew, Ragge explains, that this fresh member might become drunk before the time of the broadcast. So they hypocritically locked him up and monitored him around the clock, until the appropriate time. Ragge, in the rest of the text, seems to believe that hypocrisy is characteristic of many practices in the modern AA.

In the same vein, Archie Brodsky, Charles Bufe, and Stanton Peele are critical of the practice of many courts to mandate AA time to DUI (Driving Under the Influence) offenders, partially because there is evidence that bingeing behavior can develop in those exposed to AA. In *Resisting 12-Step Coercion: How to Fight Forced Participation in AA, NA, or 12-Step,* they say, "One very possible reason for the increase in bingeing is the emphasis in AA upon inevitable loss of control after even one drink, as codified in the AA slogan, 'one drink, one drunk'" (49). With AA as the largest of them and NA (Narcotics Anonymous) the second largest, the authors describe the prevalence of 12-Step groups as "mass phenomena in the United States. They dominate—and nearly monopolize—the addictions self-help and treatment fields" (22). AA's extensive membership makes it all the more important to certain critics that empirical analyses be ascribed to all those involved in its various processes, something which Keith Humphreys considers to be sorely lacking. In *Circles of Recovery: Self-Help Organizations for Addictions,* he says, "Policy makers, public health department heads, and healthcare administrators usually have even less understanding of mutual-help organizations than do front-line clinicians. Whether they view self-help organizations as potential collaborators, competitors, or ignorable trivia, their attitudes are rarely grounded in empirical data or extensive experience" (4). If this is the case, precautionary measures are perhaps good to keep in mind. Nonetheless, there are maybe countless individuals who have received genuinely competent guidance from these groups.

Western Philosophy and Self Help.

My undergrad was in Philosophy. I find that Donald Palmer offers a basic and lighthearted refresher of central philosophical themes in his *Looking at Philosophy: The Unbearable Heaviness of Philosophy Made Lighter.* He reminds us that Aristotle, pre-Hellenistic father of logic and proponent of Final Cause, considered each individual to be a type of enclosed teleological system. Aristotle famously gave a rudimentary explanation of this by alluding to the potentiality contained in an acorn for morphing into a grown tree (Palmer 72). Aristotle's teleology, at its core being a theory of change and self-actualization, is echoed strongly in the selections of Self Help literature which focus on activating personal potentiality.

In *The Art of Serenity,* we see fertile ground for a discussion about potentiality and purpose. T. Byram Karasu, M.D., declares in this book that personal endeavor is (a) inextricably bound with having belief in a God, and (b) a framework for self-evaluation. Though Aristotle's Prime Mover was not steeped in the Judeo-Christian tradition that Karasu at times employs in his own presentation of theological issues facing 20th Century Americans, Karasu seems to share Aristotle's caution for a "wasted life" not focused toward human virtue. Specifically, Karasu focuses a great deal on the idea of death-awareness as a tool for transformative pressure. Karasu says, "The serenity of dying… comes from sensing our nonseparateness and believing in our destiny, which is ultimately being one with nature, from which we all came" (184). It is not easy to miss here Karasu's esteem for the age-old view of a cyclic lifehood, which in his opinion only adds to the interrelated nature of personal transformative change. He touches on this by citing karmic theory and quoting from the Upanishads regarding how food represents our physical connectivity, eventually harking back to Western Philosophy to mention eternal self-recycling: "Nietzsche presented a rational premise for the idea of the Eternal Return, that if time were infinite and the particles in the universe finite, then by laws of probability all combinations must repeat themselves eternally" (179).

Other connections between Philosophy and Self Help occur when authors try to define conceptions of the Self. Butler-Bowdon believes:

> At the heart of the self-help literature are two basic conceptions of how we should see ourselves. Titles like Wayne Dyer's *Real Magic,* Thomas Moore's *Care of the Soul,* and Deepak Chopra's *The Seven Spiritual Laws of Success* assume the existence of a changeless core inside us (called variously the soul or the higher self) that guides us and helps us to fulfill a purpose unique to us. In this conception, self-knowledge is the path to maturity. Then there are titles such as Ayn Rand's *Atlas Shrugged,* Anthony Robbins' *Awaken the Giant Within,* and Benjamin Franklin's *Autobiography,*

which assume that the self is a blank slate on which you can write the story of your life (7).

Butler-Bowdon's distinction regarding Selfhood is partially a philosophical one, and its importance can be seen in Karasu's work. Karasu says, "Human beings can't imagine our own absence. The concept of nonexistence for an existent being is, at best, baffling, like endless space or other universes" (162). This statement was just one, of literally hundreds of its kind, that I noted as (explicit or implicit) attempts in Self Help texts to validate the existence of some aspect of the Self, similar to the exaltation of personal existence that Descartes made after radical doubt allowed him to open up Western Philosophy to new, unique, and challenging questions about subjectivity (Palmer 141).

I also found philosophical connections to Self Help in books pertaining to the theme of "happiness." Jonathan Haidt, a social psychologist, was one of the authors I came across who presented happiness as a complex philosophical and scientific idea. He consults many Western thinkers in his *The Happiness Hypothesis: Finding Modern Truth in Ancient Wisdom*. I was particularly interested in Haidt's mention of Epictetus. My familiarity with Epictetus is attached, in my own mind, to thinkers such as Zeno, Seneca, Marcus Aurelius, and to an entire thought movement (Stoicism) which exerted its influence during the midst of Christianity's rise. Haidt, however, weighs the methods of Epictetus against a thought movement (the Positive Psychology of the 1990's) and a slew of thinkers much less familiar to me.

He describes what "Lyubomirsky, Sheldon, Schkade, and Seligman call the 'happiness formula:' $H = S + C + V$" (91). In this model, S represents biological predisposition, C represents life conditions, and V represents one's choice of voluntary activities. Haidt says that Epictetus' cultivation of indifference to external factors fits here as one possible experimental consideration. In other words, in subjecting personal circumstances to voluntary activities aimed at reinterpretation, he ponders the feasibility of revising the formula to read $H = S + V$. He continues by exploring economic models of happiness, specifically those that employ the Scientific Method. He sharpens this discussion by defining the nature of variables and conditions that can be scrutinized under such methodologies. For instance, he explains how "the Cornell economist Robert Frank, whose 1987 book *Passions Within Reason* analyzed some of the things people do that just don't fit into economic models of pure self-interest—such as tipping in restaurants when far from home, seeking costly revenge, and staying loyal to friends and spouses when better opportunities come along" (98).

Frank's economic models of pure self-interest brought key thinkers to my mind. Firstly, though Plato's assessment of the passions is at times within the context of deconstructing the human and his government simultaneously (e.g., *The Republic*), Plato is similar to Frank in considering self-interest as being tied with the

passions. When this type of account of happiness occurs in modern Self Help, the term is often interpreted as being synonymous with pleasure. Aside from the hedonism evaluated under Hobbes, Epicurus, and Callicles, Haidt's later evaluation of pleasure as an ethical issue is mirrored in the strains between Kant's ethics and Bentham's utilitarianism. The former considers an action's intention, while the latter is commonly associated with a consequentialism that values an action based on the amount of happiness or unhappiness it causes (Palmer 203, 268). Also echoing the work of Haidt is Bentham's division of pleasure into seven categories, and even Mill's consideration of private acts in laisser-faire government, because both evaluate the economy of actions (Palmer 270, 273).

I found other contemporary counterparts to Bentham and Mill, such as Richard Layard, an economist who evaluates how actions lead to happiness or its opposite. He seems to raise questions directly to happiness researchers in addition to the common reader. For instance, in his *Happiness: Lessons from a New Science,* he highlights the "provoking idea that in the United States happiness has stagnated since 1975, while it has risen in Europe. Could this have anything to do with trends in the work-life balance?" (51). In addition to economical models such as Layard's, different (or supplemental) approaches are used by other authors to entertain questions on happiness. A few, for example, present more heavily historical analyses. Nicholas White and Darrin M. McMahon exemplify this style well. The former traces the evolution of the idea of happiness in his *A Brief History of Happiness,* and the latter sets out his own chronology in *Happiness: A History*. Both are exhaustive but of course incomplete due to the complexity of the happiness theme. McMahon admits that there remain "infinite histories of happiness to be written—histories not only of the struggles and pursuits of the peasants, slaves, apostates mentioned by Freud—but of early-modern women and late-modern aristocrats, nineteenth-century bourgeois and twentieth-century workers, conservatives and radicals, consumers and crusaders, immigrants and natives, gentiles and Jews" (xiii). Even satire is utilized as yet another approach to the notion of happiness. Will Ferguson writes an entire fictional novel, appropriately titled *Happiness,* in which the protagonist accidentally creates a new Self Help book phenomenon.

Certain treatments of the happiness theme proved especially inspiring to me personally. The medical and neuroscientific selections, specifically those that contained a major focus on the brain, helped me refine possible aspirations for my Ph.D. (I am interested in pursuing Self Help via the brain by marrying different aspects of humor therapy to neuroplasticity.) I was introduced to the concept of neuroplasticity—which refers to the physical reshaping of neural pathways—in Self Help books such as *Neural Path Therapy: How to Change Your Brain's Response to Anger, Fear, Pain and Desire,* by Matthew McKay, Ph.D., and David Harp, M.A. A main focus of my graduate work was in anxiety disorders, and I was able to find guides that spoke of these disorders with regard to neuroplasticity. In *The Mind &*

The Brain: Neuroplasticity and the Power of Mental Force, Jeffrey M. Schwartz, M.D., and Sharon Begley broach this topic by explaining, "Neuroplasticity can result not only in one region of the brain colonizing another—with remarkable effects on mental and physical function—but also in the wholesale remodeling of neural networks, of which the changes in the brains of OCD patients are only one example" (16). In *The Science of Happiness: How Our Brains Make Us Happy—and What We Can Do to Get Happier,* by Stefan Klein, Ph.D., I learned about neuroplastic events that occur during learning. He says of neuronal circuitry, "This forging of connections is called Hebbian Learning, after the Canadian psychologist Donald Hebb, who, as early as 1949, had correctly conjectured that single neurons are responsible for learning" (57).

Klein's book is an example of a text that deals with neuroplasticity less heavily than authors such as Schwartz, instead integrating other areas of brain research into the more general happiness theme. Quite a few Self Help books follow this approach. For instance, Gregory Berns, M.D., Ph.D., discusses the brain's craving for novelty in his *Satisfaction: The Science of Finding True Fulfillment,* at one point saying, "The novelty principle I've just described has been extrapolated from the observation of the way a nugget of neurons atop the brain stem functions. The more I have considered the implications of the principle, the more intrigued I have become by its potential to improve our lives" (xiv). Many "happiness" authors engage the brain by focusing on other aspects of its biochemical events. David D. Burns, M.D., author of *Feeling Good: The New Mood Therapy,* discusses the chemical landscape of neurotransmitters, saying that many of them are "categorized as 'biogenic amines' because they are manufactured from amino acids in the foods we eat" (435).

Creative/artistic evaluation of 2 clinical guides, *The Broken Mirror: Understanding and Treating Body Dysmorphic Disorder* by Katharine A. Phillips, M.D., and *The Bipolar Disorder Survival Guide* by David J. Miklowitz, Ph.D. (using Nick Mansfield's *Subjectivity: Theories of the Self from Freud to Haraway*).

In Lacanian distinctions between the imaginary and symbolic, the discussion of desire takes a prohibitory tone. Mansfield says that for Lacan, "We feel desire only because the imaginary has escaped us, because we are lost in the symbolic. In other words, the very fact that we feel desire means that we are part of the order in which desire cannot be satisfied" (46). Mansfield explains that for the Lacanian subject, symbols are directly related to immediate experience via conduits such as the experience of the Other, language, and hierarchies of meaning. Mansfield seems to believe that, for Lacan, any desire experienced in this symbolic order can translate into a sensation of lack, partially because the subject naively resolves to attain new types of Selfhood (or identities) with each desire fulfilled. Such a fulfillment is therefore, for Lacan, impossible. It leads only to new foiled attempts at finally procuring a Selfhood, in this case, of unity.

Similarly, in Phillips' interviews with Body Dysmorphia patients, it seems to me that the average patient is characterized as experiencing a fundamental rift between their sense of Selfhood and their immediate experience of themselves. Cultural and aesthetic standards such as bodily and facial symmetry appear to constitute the symbolic order to which these patients subscribe. Phillips seems to acknowledge this order as one of symptomology and language, and evaluates these two factors with tools such as the Yale-Brown Obsessive Compulsive Scale. I see Phillips as being interested in the hierarchies of subjective interpretation in her patients, specifically for which negative interpretations about body image spin the greatest severity of desire, and consequently, of lack. Phillips explains that BDD patients might even become suicidal in the midst of their self-perceived or self-conflated body image issues. Another common outcome for patients, she says, is that they pursue one cosmetic surgical procedure after another in hopes that one might finally fulfill their deepest desires for physical acceptance.

Interestingly, patients often face what I will call a phantom Other. Their physical self-evaluations rarely are reflected in the opinions of actual Others, but are instead the confabulations of unchecked subjective analysis. Phillips says, "Several men I've seen have even been turned down by hair clubs. But some people nonetheless persist in their search for a doctor who will give them what they want" (145). Unlike the self-unity that Lacanian psychoanalysts see as fueling the decision, say, to believe in a patriarchal God, BDD patients don't necessarily seem to be seeking Selfhood through a relationship with someone engaged in a shared symbolic order. Phillips instead presents BDD patients as isolated adherents to a fundamentally subjective logic—a neurosis. She says that this makes the

patient vulnerable to trigger words or situations, with little import for the origin or intent of the stressors. Phillips explains that the BDD patient may, for example, habitually reinterpret supportive evaluations as new threats to their self-esteem. This depends on each patient's level of sensitivity, both to comments that are actually intended to frustrate self-esteem and those that aren't. Phillips says, "This is sometimes referred to as the vulnerability-stress hypothesis. According to this model, in a person vulnerable to developing the disorder, stress (which for BDD might include a negative comment about appearance) can precipitate the onset of symptoms" (187).

Phillips compares BDD symptomology to clinical schemas for assessing anorexia nervosa, and in doing so, she raises sociocultural questions regarding body politics. She looks for factors that exacerbate symptoms in these two affiliated disorders, and it is clear to me that she emphasizes both the *experience* and *interpretation* of the body. This dual emphasis also occurs for Lacan, according to Mansfield. Mansfield explains, "We saw in Lacan that physical experiences like the reflection of a mirror-image in the eyeball of the other had consequences that linked the establishment of an insecure personal identity with shared structures of symbolic order" (85). Julia Kristeva, a key player in post-Lacanian psychoanalysis, relates personal participation in a Lacanian symbolic order to a system of personal identity. Mansfield explains that the identity of Kristeva's subject is extremely vulnerable to disturbances of the physical body. For example, the mere bodily feeling of uncleanliness is enough to render personal identity prone to destabilization: "*Powers of Horror* shows how the concept of abjection can be used to detect the intricate entanglement of a subjectivity-in-process and a fragile socio-symbolic order, not only in the way the body is represented but in religious systems..." (85). In addition to identity struggles in religion (such as Old Testament prohibitions), Mansfield places Kristeva in the contexts of food preparation, patriarchy, French modernism, Fascism, and Nazism. A common thread through all of Mansfield's investigations is Kristeva's insistence that the fragility of the subject is ironically tied to self-sabotage, one born from the struggle against oppressive systems. As I see it, it can also be thought of as a longing to aggravate models such as those represented by the Lacanian unified subject.

There are many instances where the fragility of identity found in a BDD patient is, just as in Kristeva's subject, susceptible to ironic paths of self-sabotage. Phillips describes patients who worsen the appearance of their face by trying to remove imperfections: "Skin picking has been described in the professional literature, particularly the dermatology literature, for many years, but it's been little researched. Traditionally, this behavior has been considered a type of 'neurotic excoriation'" (115). Phillips considers the latter term to be antiquated because it doesn't specify the cause of the behavior, which Phillips seems to regard as being bred in the hope of personal liberation and new subjectivities. Mansfield explains that for Foucault, the potential for new modes of subjectivity exists

through dynamic, at times experimental, self-creation. As is the case for the BDD patient, the self-creation of Foucault's subject can be imagined through the manipulation and interpretation of the body. Mansfield explains, "Foucault himself experimented with sado-masochism as a way of imagining new forms of selfhood that transgressed the rules of what modern discourse and its ironic police force, tabloid news culture, has laid down as acceptable sexual practice" (64).

Unlike the skin-picking of certain BDD patients, it seems that Foucault's bodily transgressions are invoked less for the promise of personal liberation and more as byproducts of power. Mansfield regularly explains that for Foucault, experimental expressions of individuality are constantly influenced and even monitored by the meaning-making power of human institutions, cultures, and governments. After all, these forces have the power to dictate the normalization and categorization of the subject. This type of normalization and categorization resonates strongly in the work of Miklowitz, the author of the second clinical guide being discussed. This second work, which presents itself as a reference on Bipolar disorder, untangles the intricacies of behavior interpretation and behavior modification in a manner at times reminiscent of Phillips' book. While doing so, Miklowitz appears to acknowledge how the powers of socialization are indistinguishable from the very modification programs that are supposed to be used to treat Bipolar patients. He even has a chapter called "What Bipolar Disorder Looks Like—to You, to the Doctors, and to Everyone Else" (13).

Both clinical guides are undeniable testaments to cultural normalization and categorization due to their reliance on tools such as the latest edition of the *Diagnostic and Statistical Manual of Mental Disorders* (DSM-IV). The DSM-IV sizes up healthy behaviors against the many checklists that evidence psychopathology—not unlike the way that homosexuality was initially categorized as an aberrant behavior worthy of clinical standing as a mental illness. Though the DSM-IV is in some sense fashioned on a rigid social and cultural consensus, it is undeniable that it provides an essential common language for practitioners. And yet, though it allows them to talk about commonly paired symptoms and therapeutic models, Phillips feels that the DSM-IV is very limited. She often describes, for example, the ambiguity in the criteria for making diagnoses. She believes that this encourages the number of cases where BDD is misdiagnosed. Similarly, Miklowitz says that the misdiagnosis of Bipolar patients is further complicated by the instances where patients do, in fact, have multiple pathologies. Miklowitz says, "The term 'comorbidity' refers to the co-occurrence of two or more psychiatric disorders in the same person. Many people have more than one DSM-IV psychiatric disorder" (44).

The intricacies of comorbidity are handled extensively in yet another text that, just as the two previously discussed, I personally implemented into my own recovery program: Sam Vaknin's *Malignant Self Love: Narcissism Revisited.* Vaknin says of individuals afflicted with narcissistic tribulations, "Depression is how such

people experience their overflowing reservoirs of aggression... Anxiety is how they experience the war raging inside them... It is very common to meet all four: a mood disorder, an anxiety disorder, an obsessive-compulsive disorder and a personality disorder in one patient" (117). Though Vaknin discusses the DSM-IV with regard to Narcissistic Personality Disorder, including the diagnostic pitfalls that face clinicians, the book style itself is less clinical. Vaknin often foregoes the step-by-step presentations of Phillips and Miklowitz in lieu of poetic prose. Vaknin's romantic language is affecting and perhaps, for some, more appropriate for discussing the emotional plane. Vaknin's narcissistic subject is characterized as a complex fallen hero, a characterization that encourages each patient to analyze himself or herself within the context of their own story.

According to Vaknin, unlike cerebral narcissists, somatic narcissists utilize their body and physical appearance to attain status and power. Though Body Dysmorphia patients are perhaps the polar opposites of vain somatic narcissists, the somatic narcissist shares many of the complexes already mentioned in my discussion of Phillips. For instance, earlier I denoted Phillips' interest in BDD patients' severity of desire (in quantifiable levels), and consequently, their sensation of lack. Vaknin's somatic narcissists are similarly unsatiated, obsessively and pathologically seeking to find outside validation for their level of desirability to others. Sexual conquests, he explains, are perhaps the most common means of self-evaluation for this type of narcissist; other narcissists also experience unhealthy desire, such as the cerebral narcissist, who tirelessly seeks to overpower and impress others with knowledge or intellectual prowess.

Earlier I highlighted the normalization and categorization of the subject in the work of both Phillips and Miklowitz. Vaknin is highly aware of the forces of socialization, often shaping narcissism as a volatile reaction to the expectations of social and group polity. Though narcissists do not accommodate easily to certain aspects of shared culture, just as the BDD or Bipolar patient, they show many less signs of socialization oppression than both. They may cope, for instance, through the reappropriation of social power. By cultivating a different kind of social sensitivity—one employed for the sake of manipulation—Vaknin says that the narcissistic subject attempts to shift the dynamic of influence in favor of their own needs and desires. He describes how social ploys can, for instance, be used by the narcissist to consciously perpetuate a very specific personal image. Unfortunately, such attempts meet with varying degrees of success. Vaknin explains that, at times, they alienate the very audience which is meant to be swayed: "The very people who are supposed to sustain his grandiose fantasies through their adoration and attention – mostly find him too repulsive, eccentric (weird) or dangerous to interact with" (197). This irony is reminiscent of Phillips' patients who deform their own faces in a failed attempt to make themselves attractive.

Other evaluators of the Self Help industry.

With such a psychotherapeutic focus in the Self Help historical outline earlier, it is important to note that not all contemporary Self Help authors implement tools from Psychology similarly. While certain authors trace emotional defense mechanisms back to early childhood, claiming that the rearing environment was likely infused with different types of abuse, others contest. Steve Salerno, author of *SHAM: How the Self-Help Movement Made America Helpless,* says, "It's easy to scream abuse when the term is defined so vaguely and generically as to include just about anything. It's easier still when the culture tells you that you would have turned out just fine had your parents not destroyed your 'essential self' by trying to mold you into a tractable, well-mannered citizen" (138). Salerno is not advocating a denial to the existence of child abuse, of course, but calls for healthy skepticism. Admittedly, though certain Self Help authors describe specific types of parental behavior that might induce negative development, there is sometimes very limited guidance for how to separate these from rearing tactics that resemble but don't necessarily constitute abusive rearing. Salerno comments on mental health Self Help books by pointing out their growing emphasis on victimization status. Victimization, he says, primes us to extract an interpretation of abuse from where there was none to begin with. He reinforces this point by mentioning "titles of the movement's signature works: *Toxic Parents: Overcoming Their Hurtful Legacy and Reclaiming Your Life, The Doormat Syndrome,* and *Raising Children in a Socially Toxic Environment.*" He continues, "If you're in decent shape yourself, there's always the problem of interacting with the dysfunctionals around you: *Toxic Coworkers: How to Deal with Dysfunctional People on the Job; Coping with Toxic Managers, Subordinates, and Other Difficult People"* (139).

Salerno is not alone in his contempt for certain aspects of the industry. Stewart Justman, in his *Fool's Paradise: The Unreal World of Pop Psychology,* declares, "Self-help writers make sweeping accusations as health propositions. A genre that disparages judgment, turning the very word into an epithet, makes the most venomous judgments freely. A genre that intones the beauty of growth retails juvenile views and resentments" (19). Both Salerno and Justman are deft at underscoring the often overlooked contradictions in modern Self Help works. Their critiques are historical, sociological, and philosophical. Justman, for instance, explains that his book "traces the inspiration of the pop psychology movement to the utopianism of the 1960's and argues that it consistently misuses the rhetoric of civil rights" (vii).

Justman's contrasting of Self Help to the mechanics of social movements, as well as Salerno's cautions about victimization, both find fairly obvious reverberations in a third evaluator of the industry, Micki McGee. McGee, author of *Self Help, Inc.,* says that a "politics of victimization requires good guys and bad guys, and historically it has been all too easy for one exploited group to imagine

another exploited group as its oppressor" (182). Just as Salerno promotes healthy skepticism regarding issues of say, child abuse, without necessarily espousing a call to ignore genuine cases of abuse, McGee is not advocating a cessation of efforts toward social reform. Instead, she wants to emphasize the limits of operating change from and structuring empowerment on a politics of victimhood. This precaution, in her view, can actually aid to counter social inequity because it shifts focus from the victim to a more complete understanding of the oppression itself. She believes that, unfortunately, this doesn't always occur. She says, "Even the most visible social justice movements of the late twentieth century have tended to eschew struggles over the distribution of goods and resources, focusing instead on issues that involve symbolic or representational issues (sexist or racist representations, for example)" (184). She is particularly interested in the oppression experienced by the lowest rungs of the American labor force, sometimes alluding to the way that self-improvement operates on the belief that wealth necessarily signifies industry and competence, whereas poverty is instead seen as a marker of laziness or stupidity. I, just as she, believe that capitalistic realities cannot be denied as possible deterrents to self-actualization. Even the work of Maslow, who popularized the self-actualization term, considers that its pursuit is rendered futile without some measure of economic security.

Steven Starker, the earlier mentioned author of *Oracle at the Supermarket: The American Preoccupation with Self-Help Books,* notes that cost also plays a role in the appeal of purchasing Self Help books. They frequently promise complete success for mere dollars as opposed to the higher expense of psychologists and similar counselors. He says of these mental health professionals, "Despite the expense, they seldom offer any promises of success; most are prohibited from doing so by the ethical codes of their respective professions" (5). Though Starker does not consider Self Help books as replacements for professional sources of consultation, he believes that health care practitioners and social scientists can no longer responsibly ignore these books because they have become so accommodated into the larger culture. Starker says, "We need to identify and briefly consider some of the major criticisms that have been leveled against the self-help genre as a whole, and against subcategories of it" (157). Starker himself sorts through the anti-intellectual claims against New Thought, pediatricians who complain about the failure of many child-care books to consider extenuating circumstances, the inaccuracies of certain nutritional works, and the recommendations made by researchers for a structured method of book evaluation. Starker explains, "Glasgow and Rosen have recommended that all commercially published self-help books contain a standardized introductory page reporting on the number and types of subjects tested with the manual, the conditions of testing, the percentage of subjects completing the program, the immediate and long-term results, predictors of treatment outcome, and so on" (165). Starker presents Russell Glasgow and Gerald Rosen as two psychologists

who reviewed programs ranging from weight reduction guides to behavioral modification treatments for phobias. Their suggestions, however, have largely been ignored. Starker feels that the average consumer would benefit little from the kind of details lobbied for by the two psychologists, foremost because the reader is likely a non-psychologist.

Steve Salerno's *SHAM* expends much of its energy focusing on personalities of the industry, particularly the circumstances of each guru's ascendancy. Furthermore, Salerno attempts to poke holes in the greater market, sometimes noting the incongruity of emphasizing self-reliance while building empires on the repeat business of customers. While Salerno often accuses the industry of steering readers consciously and viciously, Starker is in certain ways sensitive to social context. Starker explains that many trends in the industry's book sales relate directly to contemporary cultural phenomena. He goes through different decades, such as when he discusses the sexually informative works in the 1920's that reflected how Victorian repression had begun to give way to the disinhibition of the Jazz Age. Other examples include soldiers' handbooks that were created during the high idealism of World War I.

While McGee can at times be as deeply sociocultural as Starker, she maintains an emphasis on Self Help's reflection of economic realities. She theorizes that a gendered split occurred in Self Help literature at the outset of the 1980's because "women were entering the labor force in increasing numbers and asserting the self-interested individuality that had once been primarily the prerogative of men" (81). She contends that much Self Help for women of this period relied on the introduction of market values into ordinary life. In addition to presenting series of "solutions," she notes that many of these books alluded to competition and winning. However, McGee argues that the feminization of Self Help allowed a transition from showing how individuals might navigate a free market of opportunities, to a reinterpretation of competition itself. For McGee, self-fulfillment need not be a game with one against another, but is by nature a cooperative game where an individual competes against herself. She explores other common metaphors used by women's Self Help literature of the period, such as "upward mobility" and the notion of imagining one's life as a business enterprise. McGee points out that Helen Gurley Brown recommended "keeping tabs on one's emotional investments and balances five years in advance of Stephen R. Covey's introduction of the idea of an 'emotional bank account'" (85).

Starker is also interested in the effect of economic realities on Self Help. He believes that, in the 1980's, there was "a reaction by the American business community to the widespread perception that it had been badly outclassed by the Japanese" (144), which caused an influx of business literature meant to alleviate a hurt American pride. Starker also considers this the first time that Self Help began to have its characteristic emphasis on the idea of excellence: "In the 1980's, for example, readers suddenly became fascinated with 'excellence,' flocking to such

works as *In Search of Excellence* (1982) by Thomas J. Peters and Robert H. Waterman, Jr., *Creating Excellence* (1984) by Craig R. Hickman and Michael A. Silva, and *A Passion for Excellence* (1985) by Thomas J. Peters and Nancy K. Austin" (144). Starker believes that the Self Help of the 80's especially responded to the nature of struggle and uncertainty of the times, creating an enhanced awareness of life's physical and economic limitations.

Regarding personal limitations, Justman feels that Self Help books are poor guides. He says, "If, as I will argue, the theory that we can transform ourselves completely—the animating promise of the self-help movement—is questionable, still more so is the notion that we can transform ourselves overnight, as if our own Year One had been instantly realized or a switch were thrown and a current of healing energy flowed" (101). Promises of quick and total transformation, in his view, exacerbate feelings of hopelessness and frustration that inevitably arise for the millions of readers who are unable to attain such change. He says, "To wit, if you make people believe they have full control over their lives, and then their lives don't get better (or even get worse), how could that *not* throw their synapses into turmoil?" (250).

Tom Tiede is another author who discusses the problematic nature of Self Help's quick-fixes, as exemplified by his *Self-Help Nation: The Long Overdue, Entirely Justified, Delightfully Hostile Guide to the Snake-Oil Peddlers Who Are Sapping Our Nation's Soul.* He candidly opines, "Few believe any longer that people can be herded into jurisdictional purification, but the longing for perfectibility, at least in the American ranks, has become damn near a democratic demand" (8). As part of her unfavorable critique of the industry, Wendy Kaminer discusses the promises of transformation within the spiritual realm. In *I'm Dysfunctional, You're Dysfunctional: The Recovery Movement and Other Self-Help Fashions,* Kaminer says that in "the margins of denominational religion, from New Thought and Christian Science to New Age, spiritualism has sought credibility in pseudoscience, describing the magic of cosmic energy while borrowing from new theories about the human psyche and the power of imagination" (124). Both Kaminer and Tiede consider even the act of purchasing a Self Help book objectionable. Kaminer says, "Merely buying a self-help book is an act of dependence, a refusal to confront the complexities of a solitary creative act and to endure the loneliness and failures that are the price of its surprises" (165). Similarly, Tiede says, "I urge you to go to the forest for succor instead of the bookshop" (224).

In addition to the Self Help evaluators already discussed, who provide more general critiques of Self Help, other types of writers have scrutinized the industry. David Riklan is an example of a researcher who focuses less on constructing social commentaries, instead aiming more for the compilation and organization of the Self Help texts and authors themselves. Riklan is the author of *Self Improvement: The Top 101 Experts Who Help Us Improve Our Lives.* Riklan outlines the following areas in Self Improvement: "Personal Empowerment, Spirituality,

Business, Relationships, Personal Finance, and Professional & Academic Skills" (9). Besides Self Help subject categories such as those used by Riklan, I devised my own basic division of Self Help books, based on empirical value, which could be designated as follows: (a) Specialized books, usually meant for the professionals of a particular occupation or academic field, (b) texts that simplify or clarify specialized subject material in an attempt to make the material accessible to a wider readership, and (c) "cure-all" and "quick-fix" selections, which, depending on the particular book, might lack depth or a strong scientific grounding.

Allow me to explain the above schema. I think it is important to emphasize that the level of discussion is different in each Self Help book—not all of them are written for total laypeople. For instance, there are countless guides to the different reissues of the DSM, such as James Morrison's *DSM-IV Made Easy*. In addition to medical sources such as the DSM, other examples point to a tradition in Self Help literature of simplifying or clarifying specialized language for the sake of reaching wider audiences. In *D.I.Y.: Design it Yourself,* Ellen Lupton explains that her book "demystifies the technical side of small-scale publishing in various media while opening up your mind to the creative side of design" (17). An insurance expert named Kimberly Lankford cuts through some of the industry jargon for her readers in *The Insurance Maze: How You Can Save Money on Insurance—and Still Get the Coverage You Need*. She says, "Despite the doomsday headlines about soaring health insurance costs, many people can get surprisingly good deals if they know how to make the most of their employers' options or shop around for a policy on their own" (viii). Lyle Wilkinson covers financial issues in *DIY Portfolio Management*. He says, "Investing your money in security instruments can be an expensive way to gain a portfolio management education. Studying investing/trading books can help reduce the time and cost of your education" (9).

In the end, though a Self Help book might lack depth or breadth on a particular theme, I believe that a conscious pulling of sources from different areas has the potential to not only remedy this recurring deficit, but to also underscore the broader challenge to produce genuinely insightful, informative, and effective personal transformation material. (For the sake of assortment in my own research, I made sure to consult sources ranging from "easy" to "hard"—including some intended for professionals.) In essence, I am not trying to write a defense of the entire industry. In fact, I personally have distaste for the work of many Self Help authors, regardless of their undeniable influence on thousands of people. Yet, I have left with the basic conviction that while this particular industry is in need of improvement, it nonetheless deserves attention. I see boundless potential for positive reform. Finally, it is important to note that I am not claiming to have simply cured myself with Self Help books—I have, after all, the ability for extreme self-discipline. Instead, each book was used as a supplement, consciously and carefully, to a greater Self Help program of my own design. Indeed, diligence and common sense are incredibly important tools to use in any exploration of the

United States' fascinating, evolving, and culturally significant Self Help industry. Simply put, read Self Help with a critical eye.

The goal of my self-designed Master's Degree was to describe and help co-create an emerging academic field of Self Help by establishing a possible set of foundations for its developing epistemology. Despite the fact that I chose to work in a somewhat quirky area of study—and despite the fact that I pulled my pants down and exposed my penis during my final presentation for students and faculty—I nonetheless addressed the degree criteria over the course of all my work. For instance, I articulated historical and cultural influences on my chosen area of study by acknowledging the antecedents of Self Help. I familiarized myself with data, methods, theories, and analyses pertaining to my area of inquiry, including their claims to authenticity (scientific or otherwise). However, I also demonstrated non-traditional forms of learning. For example, particularly relevant to my style of research is the fact that I managed to integrate both theory and practice. The former I accomplished in both my book and academic work, while the latter was addressed through the development of my own sophisticated cognitive behavioral therapy and Self Help programs.

Addendum to March 2007 letter at end of main book, as written by Ryan T. (That letter was written in response to an earlier version of this book; also, the Appendix had not yet been added.)

(September 2007)

Al's efforts to "relax" into his true self continue, and the latest draft of the book reflects this. The posturing and off-putting tone of which I wrote before has mostly evaporated, and the real him is much more evident throughout. As always, the speed of his progress amazes me. I've never seen anyone do what he has done.

I've told him I think the book could benefit from a more defined structure and a detailed, chronological account of his self-treatments, but otherwise I love it, and the less-structured form clearly serves to illustrate something of his inner clamor. I'm extremely proud of what he has accomplished.

Signed,

Ryan T.

Miscellaneous notes.

*As an academic memoir, this book was meant to be: (a) entertaining, and (b) educational.

*Though my evaluation was of the American Self Help industry, I do acknowledge that I occasionally consulted texts that originated outside of the United States.

*Certain sub-facets in the fields of Psychology and Western Philosophy were much more familiar to me—especially during my undergraduate program, when I was immersed in the stuff—compared to my understandings of Neuroscience, at which I am a mere novice.

*Journal entries were edited down for length; other small adjustments were made as well.

*I deeply regret if the animal exploitation mentioned in this book was either frightening or infuriating to you. I wrestled with whether or not to mention it, and in the end I felt that omitting it would leave my life story less complete. I remind you that I was still a child at the time, and that my judgment was certainly lacking. Also, I should explain that the exploitative instances were very few and relatively minor. Currently, **I do not support animal cruelty of any kind!!!** In fact, animals are one of the greatest joys in my life today. I frequently make it a priority to visit the puppies during my lunch break.

*My family, especially my parents, will understandably be very embarrassed of my self-disclosure in this book; I hereby absolve them of any official endorsement of my work. As a 25 year old adult, the decision to write it is mine and mine alone.

*I think that Ryan is overly optimistic about my recovery. I can tell you from here in the cockpit, from here on the front lines, that I still struggle intensely, so intensely, daily. With trillions of needles in my soul. But I must admit that I'm way better than before. There's no comparison. Like day and night.

*Please refer to my website for any updates, clarifications, or corrections.

*And on a final note: These days I've been learning a little bit of professionalism. I actively try to avoid being rude, instead aspiring to a greater degree of diplomacy in my interactions with other people.

ENDNOTES

[i] In this citation there are three dots (...) to indicate an extraction, specifically where the sentence is shortened—literally cut off, but in no way reworded—from its entirety as in the original text. Elsewhere in this book, three dots will be used to indicate similar extractions. This only applies to quotations, not when it is done in my own writing.

[ii] Though no other author surveying the industry uses this specific list of 13 names, I consulted other general evaluators of the industry to ensure that I had not overlooked some of the most influential predecessors of contemporary American Self Help. And yet, I chose to eliminate some of the most acclaimed personalities. I was simply less drawn to certain authors. Also, in order to focus on the 13 men without breaking up the timeline of the historical presentation, I will forego extensively discussing critiques of their work. Each of the 13, certainly, has vehement detractors and outspoken critics. However, instead of focusing on specific objections to each, I wish to constrain this kind of debate to critics who analyze the industry as a whole. This will take place in a later portion of this Appendix.

[iii] Regarding the form which Protestantism's prescriptive guidelines have taken throughout its history, Kevin Phillips, author of *American Theocracy: The Peril and Politics of Radical Religion, Oil, and Borrowed Money in the 21st Century,* says, "Christianity in the United States, especially Protestantism, has always had an evangelical—which is to say,

missionary—and frequently a radical or combative streak. Some message has always had to be preached, punched, or proselytized" (100).

[iv] The way that these movements arose against the backdrop of traditional denominations is reminiscent of the sectarian revivalism which Kevin Phillips considers a main feature of American religion. In *American Theocracy,* he says, "Even by the time of the American Revolution the old colonial elite denominations—Congregationalists in New England, Quakers in Pennsylvania, and Anglicans from Chesapeake Bay and to the south—were in places being challenged or overtaken by upstart Baptists and Scotch-Irish Presbyterians" (107).

[v] Peale's pushing of Christianity stood in contrast, say, to the type of activity resulting from sects and doomsday prophecies. In *American Theocracy,* Kevin Phillips describes the latter as phenomena interesting enough to receive even international attention. He says, "Over the years, new waves of fervor, zeal, and agitation—from quakes, shakes, and jerks to millennial watch keeping and speaking in tongues—have sparked almost continuous cultural and behavioral comment from domestic and foreign observers" (105).

[vi] Maslow was able to explore concepts in Humanistic Psychology and self-actualization as an early associate of the Esalen Institute. In her "Cults and Cosmic Consciousness" piece, Paglia describes Esalen as having been heavily influenced by George Gurdjieff, who created a mixture of Tantric Buddhism, Hinduism, and Sufi mysticism. She says that

Esalen's "workshops, based on the Gurdjieff group session, drew a long list of writers and thinkers in the sixties, including Alan Watts and Aldous Huxley" (v10, n3, sec-9).

[vii] Though Covey may have been the foremost psychologist of the 60's, late in the decade other less mainstream thinkers began to develop momentum. In her "Cults and Cosmic Consciousness" piece, Paglia explains that Werner Erhard investigated Zen and other schools of thought in the late 60's, eventually founding EST (Erhard Seminar Training) in 1971. Paglia describes the nature of EST, including the extreme conditions to which participants were subject: "Marathon, eight-hour sessions, in which they were confined and harassed, supposedly led to the breakdown of conventional ego, after which they were in effect born again. Erhard said he wanted 'to blow the Mind' in the sixties way. Explicitly anti-Christian in philosophy, EST was generally regarded as a cult, but it was a private, for-profit organization" (v10, n3, sec-9).

[viii] Though the New Age movement began to form in the late 70's, it was during this time, in the 80's, that it was recognized in earnest. In her "Cults and Cosmic Consciousness" piece, Paglia explains that New Age is expansive and difficult to pin down, but that one main theme running through New Age belief and practice is an idea that it inherited from the 60's: cosmic consciousness. Paglia says that this notion was different in the 60's because it was often tied to a desire to shatter social convention, while in the 70's it was more specifically concerned with afterlife issues, such as reincarnation, past lives, and astral projection. New Age is profoundly important to the discussion of Self Help because many writers in the industry, including many in this

timeline, were either influenced by or part of some aspect of New Age. Many writers share New Age's reverence, for instance, for a spiritual dimension which transcends the visible, material one. Furthermore, New Age is often associated with alternative medicine (such as that practiced by Deepak Chopra) and NLP (which, as discussed earlier, influenced writers such as Carnegie).

Regarding the origin of New Age, Paglia points to two women of the 19th Century: Mary Eddy and Helena Blavatsky. Paglia says that Eddy "believed she had recovered from chronic invalidism through New Thought, the mental-health philosophy of Phineas Parkhurst Quimby, with whom she studied in Maine. In the 1840's, Quimby had fused Hindu and Buddhist concepts from Transcendentalism with hypnotherapy, based on Anton Mesmer's eighteenth-century theory of 'animal magnetism'" (v10, n3, sec-9). Paglia explains that Eddy accepted Christianity, as contrasted with Quimby, and that she founded Christian Science (which says that the power to heal belongs to divine sources, not physicians or medicine). Similarly, Blavatsky also founded her own movement. Paglia explains, "Madame Blavatsky claimed to have acquired secret knowledge through seven years of study in Tibet. In New York in 1875, she and Henry Steele Olcott founded the Theosophical Society, which combined Hindu and Buddhist concepts with the Western esoteric tradition" (v10, n3, sec-9). Blavatsky declared that all religions potentially held portions of truth about the universe, and Paglia explains that Blavatsky even tried to unify world religions (through their shared mysticism) in her two major works: *Isis Unveiled* and *The Secret Doctrine.*

[ix] The sales of certain Self Help books dipped in the early part of this decade. In her "Finding Help on the Shelves" piece for *Publishers Weekly,* Marcia Ford explains that in the "Christian market, the category underwent a decided overhaul in the late 1990s after enjoying self-help heydays in the 1980s... In the early '90s, classic self-help books began suffering a decline, according to Lyn Cryderman, Zondervan v-p and publisher... 'Many of these titles were simplistic and promised more than they could deliver. Consumers realize that most of life's problems cannot be solved in seven steps,' he says. 'They want help with life's challenges, but they prefer to put their trust in authors who provide more than answers.' He cited as an example Mike Yaconelli's 'Messy Spirituality'—a book whose title alone offers a fairly clear idea of just how the category has changed" (S2, S4).

[x] Joanna Macy—with an international following over the course of 40 years as a speaker of Buddhist philosophy and ecology movements—is another example of someone who has popularized Eastern thought in the United States. In *World as Lover, World as Self,* she explains that a factor in "aiding in the dismantling of the ego-self and the creation of the eco-self is the resurgence of nondualistic spiritualities. Buddhism is distinctive in the clarity and sophistication with which it deals with the constructs and the dynamics of self" (189). Macy believes that Buddhism stands in comparison to systems theory because both undermine categorical distinctions between self and other.

Works cited

Berns, Gregory. *Satisfaction: The Science of Finding True Fulfillment.* New York: Hendry Holt and Company, LLC., 2005.

Behrman, Andy. *Electroboy: A Memoir of Mania.* New York: Random House Trade Paperbacks, 2003.

Bremner, Robert H. *American Philanthropy.* Illinois: University of Chicago Press, 1988.

Brodsky, Archie and Bufe, Charles and Peele, Stanton. *Resisting 12-Step Coercion: How to Fight Forced Participation in AA, NA, or 12-Step.* Arizona: See Sharp Press, 2000.

Burns, David D. *Feeling Good: The New Mood Therapy.* New York: Avon Books, 1999.

Butler-Bowdon. *50 Self-Help Classics: 50 Inspirational Books to Transform Your Life.* London: Nicholas Brealey Publishing, 2003.

Carnegie, Dale. *How to Stop Worrying and Start Living.* New York: Pocket Books, 2004.

Carnegie, Dale. *How to Win Friends and Influence People.* New York: Pocket Books, 1998.

Chopra, Deepak. *Ageless Body, Timeless Mind: The Quantum Alternative to Growing Old.* New York: Three Rivers Press, 1998.

Chopra, Deepak. *Creating Affluence: The A-to-Z Steps to a Richer Life.* California: Amber-Allen Publishing, Inc., 1998

Chopra, Deepak. *The Path to Love: Spiritual Strategies for Healing.* New York: Three Rivers Press, 1998.

Covey, Stephen R. *Principle Centered Leadership.* New York: Simon & Schuster, 1992.

Covey, Stephen R. *Seven Habits of Highly Effective People: Powerful Lessons in Personal Change.* New York: Simon & Schuster, 1989.

Covey, Stephen M.R. *The SPEED of Trust: The One Thing that Changes Everything.* New York: Simon & Schuster, 2006.

Davidson, Jonathan and Dreher, Henry. *The Anxiety Book.* New York: Riverhead Books, 2003.

Dembling, Sophia and Gutierrez, Lisa. *The Making of Dr. Phil: The Straight-Talking True Story of Everyone's Favorite Therapist.* New Jersey: Wiley & Sons, Inc., 2004.

Duke, Patty. *Call Me Anna: The Autobiography of Patty Duke.* New York: Bantam Books, 1988.

Elder, Charles. (Book review.) *The Permanente Journal.* Winter 2004. v8 n1.

Ford, Marcia. "Finding Help on the Shelves." *Publishers Weekly.* May 23, 2005. v252 n21.

Franklin, Benjamin. *Poor Richard's Almanack.* New York: Barnes & Noble Publishing, Inc., 2004.

Geldard, Richard G. *The Essential Transcendentalists.* New York: Penguin Group, Inc., 2005.

Gerzon, Robert. *Finding Serenity in the Age of Anxiety.* New York: Bantam Books, 1998.

Haidt, Jonathan. *The Happiness Hypothesis: Finding Modern Truth in Ancient Wisdom.* New York: Basic Books, 2006.

Henderson, J. Adrienne. *Don't Worry.* New York: Dodd, Mead and Company, 1981.

Humphreys, Keith. *Circles of Recovery: Self-Help Organizations for Addictions.* Cambridge: Cambridge University Press, 2004.

Isaacson, Walter. *Benjamin Franklin: An American Life.* New York: Simon & Schuster, 2003.

James, William. *Pragmatism: A New Name for Some Old Ways of Thinking.* Utah: Walking Lion Press, 2006.

James, William. *Psychology: The Briefer Course.* New York: Dover Publications, 2001.

Jamison, Kay R. *An Unquiet Mind: A Memoir of Moods and Madness.* New York: Vintage Books, 1997.

Justman, Stewart. *Fool's Paradise: The Unreal World of Pop Psychology.* Illinois: Ivan R. Dee, 2005.

Kaminer, Wendy. *I'm Dysfunctional, You're Dysfunctional: The Recovery Movement and Other Self-Help Fashions.* New York: Vintage Books, 1993.

Karasu, T. Byram. *The Art of Serenity.* New York: Simon & Schuster, 2003.

Kaysen, Susanna. *Girl, Interrupted.* New York: Vintage Books, 1994.

Klein, Stefan. *The Science of Happiness.* New York: Marlowe & Company, 2002.

Lankford, Kimberly. *The Insurance Maze: How You Can Save Money on Insurance--and Still Get the Coverage You Need.* New York: Kaplan Publishing, 2006.

Layard, Richard. *Happiness: Lessons from a New Science.* New York: The Penguin Press, 2005.

Leahy, Robert. *Cognitive Therapy Techniques: A Practitioner's Guide.* New York: The Guilford Press, 2003.

Lupton, Ellen. *D.I.Y.: Design it Yourself.* New York: Princeton Architectural Press, 2006.

Macy, Joanna. *World as Lover, World as Self.* California: Parallax Press, 1991.

Mansfield, Nick. *Subjectivity: Theories of the Self from Freud to Haraway.* New York: New York University Press, 2000.

Maslow, Abraham. *Maslow on Management.* New York: John Wiley and Sons, Inc., 1998.

Maslow, Abraham. *Toward a Psychology of Being.* New York: John Wiley and Sons, Inc., 1999.

McGee, Micki. *Self-Help, Inc.* Oxford: Oxford University Press, 2005.

McGraw, Phillip. *Life Strategies: Doing What Works, Doing What Matters.* New York: Hyperion, 1999.

McGraw, Phillip. *Relationship Rescue.* New York: Hyperion, 2000.

McGraw, Phillip. *The Self Matters Companion: Helping You Create Your Life from the Inside Out.* New York: Simon & Schuster, Inc., 2002.

McMahon, Darrin M. *Happiness: A History.* New York: Atlantic Monthly Press, 2006.

Miklowitz, David J. *The Bipolar Disorder Survival Guide.* New York: The Guilford Press, 2002.

Miller, Alice. *The Drama of the Gifted Child: The Search for the True Self.* New York: Basic Books, 1997.

Norem, Julie. *The Positive Power of Negative Thinking.* New York: Basic Books, 2001.

Paglia, Camille. "Cults and Cosmic Consciousness: Religious Vision in the American 1960's." *Arion: A Journal of Humanities and Classics.* Winter 2003. v10 n3.

Palmer, Donald. *Looking at Philosophy: The Unbearable Heaviness of Philosophy Made Lighter.* California: Mayfield Publishing Company, 1994.

Peale, Norman V. *The Power of Positive Thinking.* New York: Ballantine Books, 1996.

Peale, Norman V. *You Can If You Think You Can.* New York: Simon & Schuster, 1987.

Phillips, Katharine A. *The Broken Mirror: Understanding and Treating Body Dysmorphic Disorder.* Oxford: Oxford University Press, 1986.

Phillips, Kevin. *American Theocracy: The Peril and Politics of Radical Religion, Oil, and Borrowed Money in the 21st Century.* New York: Penguin Group, Inc., 2006.

Quinodoz, Jean-Michel. *Reading Freud: A Chronological Exploration of Freud's Writings.* East Sussex: Routledge, 2005.

Ragge, Ken. *The Real AA: Behind the Myth of 12-Step Recovery.* Arizona: See Sharp Press, 1997.

Rieff, Philip. *Freud: The Mind of the Moralist.* Illinois: Chicago University Press, 1979.

Riklan, David. *Self Improvement: The Top 101 Experts Who Help Us Improve Our Lives.* New Jersey: Self Improvement Online, Inc., 2004.

Rivera, Hugo and Villepigue, James. *The Body Sculpting Bible for Men.* New York: Hatherleigh Press, 2004.

Robbins, Anthony. *Awaken the Giant Within: How to Take Immediate Control of Your Mental, Emotional, Physical, and Financial Destiny!* New York: Simon & Schuster, 2003.

Robbins, Anthony. *Giant Steps: Small Changes to Make a Big Difference.* New York: Simon & Schuster, 1994.

Robbins, Anthony. *Unlimited Power: The New Science of Personal Achievement.* New York: Simon & Schuster, 1997.

Robinson, David M. *Natural Life: Thoreau's Worldly Transcendentalism.* New York: Cornell University Press, 2004.

Rogers, Carl. *A Way of Being.* New York: Houghton Mufflin Company, 1995.

Rogers, Carl. *On Becoming a Person: A Therapist's View of Psychotherapy.* New York: Houghton Mifflin Company, 1995.

Ryan, M.J. *Attitudes of Gratitude.* California: Conari Press, 1999.

Salerno, Steve. *SHAM: How the Self-Help Movement Made America Helpless.* New York: Crown Publishers, 2005.

Sant, Tom. *The Giants of Sales.* New York: AMACOM, 2006.

Schunk, Dale H. and Zimmerman, Barry J. *Self-Regulation of Learning and Performance: Issues and Educational Applications.* New Jersey: Lawrence Erlbaum Associates, Inc., 1994.

Schwartz, Jeffrey M. and Begley, Sharon. *The Mind & The Brain: Neuroplasticity and the Power of Mental Force.* New York: HarperCollins Publishers, 2003.

Starker, Steven. *Oracle at the Supermarket: The American Preoccupation with Self-Help Books.* New Jersey: Transaction Publishers, 2002.

Styron, William. *Darkness Visible: A Memoir of Madness.* New York: Vintage Books, 1992.

Tiede, Tom. *Self-Help Nation: The Long Overdue, Entirely Justified, Delightfully Hostile Guide to the Snake-Oil Peddlers Who Are Sapping Our Nation's Soul.* New York: Atlantic Monthly Press, 2001.

Vaknin, Sam. *Malignant Self Love: Narcissism Revisited.* Skopje: Narcissus Publications, 2005.

Weiss, Richard. *The American Myth of Success: From Horatio Alger to Norman Vincent Peale.* Illinois: University of Illinois Press, 1988.

Wilkinson, Lyle. *DIY Portfolio Management.* Hawaii: Selact Publishing, 2003.

Wurtzel, Elizabeth. *Prozac Nation.* New York: Penguin Group Inc., 1995.

*The dates of birth (and, if applicable, death) of the men in the historical outline were obtained from www.Wikipedia.org

www.ingramcontent.com/pod-product-compliance
Ingram Content Group UK Ltd.
Pitfield, Milton Keynes, MK11 3LW, UK
UKHW051129260726
13967UKWH00010B/2951

9 781412 089036